CULTURE AND
COMMITMENT

Margaret Mead

CULTURE AND COMMITMENT

The New Relationships
Between the Generations
in the 1970s

REVISED AND UPDATED EDITION

Columbia University Press
New York
1978

Columbia University Press
Copyright © 1970, 1978 by Margaret Mead
All rights reserved

LIBRARY OF CONGRESS CATALOGING IN PUBLICATION DATA
Mead, Margaret, 1901-
   Culture and commitment.

   Bibliography: p.
   Includes index.
   1. Culture.   2. Social change.   3. Conflict of
generations.   I. Title.
HM101.M38   1978b   301.2   78-14589
ISBN 0-231-04632-4

Published by arrangement with Doubleday & Co., Inc. *Culture
and Commitment* was originally published by The Natural
History Press/Doubleday & Co., Inc., in 1970, in hardcover
and paperback.

Printed in the United States of America

ACKNOWLEDGMENTS

Grateful acknowledgment is made to the National Institute for
Mental Health, Research Grant NIMH MN-03303-09, "The Factor
of Mental Health in Allopsychic Orientation," and Research Grant
NIMH 07675-06, "Cultural Systematics in New Guinea"; to The
National Science Foundation, Research Grant NSF GS-642, "The
Cultural Structure of Imagery"; and to the Jane Belo Tannenbaum
Fund of The American Museum of Natural History.

The poem *And Your Young Men Shall See Visions* was published in *The City Day,* edited by Eda Lou Walton (New York:
Ronald Press, 1929, p. 95), and *For Mary Catherine Bateson* was
first published in my autobiography, *Blackberry Winter: My
Earlier Years* (New York: Morrow, 1972, p. 272).

I owe the essay written by a fifteen-year-old Texan boy (pp.
74–75) and the 1977 epilogue to that essay (pp. 107–8) to Shannon Dickson.

Thanks are also due to Pat Overby, Donald Sparks, and Jim
Stein for portions of their freshman essays on "The Generation
Gap."

For criticism, I am grateful to Mary Catherine Bateson and
Geoffrey Gorer for Part II and to Rhoda Metraux for Part I; for
over-all editing to Susan Haven; and for periodic editorial en-
couragement to Elizabeth Frost Knappman.

To
My father's mother
and
My daughter's daughter

Biographical Note

Since 1925, when she began her pioneering field work with primitive peoples of the South Pacific, Margaret Mead has been uninterruptedly involved in the study of man's cultural evolution.

Born in Philadelphia in 1901, Margaret Mead was educated at Barnard College and Columbia University. At the age of twenty-three, after completing her graduate work in anthropology, she spent nine months living with and studying the isolated inhabitants of American Samoa. Her research resulted in the classic *Coming of Age in Samoa*, originally published in 1928. In 1926 she became a member of the staff of The American Museum of Natural History and began a long series of studies of different parts of the Pacific—to fill out her knowledge of the Pacific cultures that were her responsibility at the Museum—and to enlarge our knowledge of different aspects of human life. In 1925–26 she studied adolescence in Samoa; in 1928–29 she studied early childhood among the Manus, followed by studies of male and female differences and infant development in three New Guinea tribes. Her findings were published in *Sex and Temperament in Three Primitive Societies* (1936) and *Male and Female* (1949). She did similar studies in Bali and New Guinea from 1936–39.

After the birth of her daughter in 1939, Margaret Mead devoted ten years to the application of anthropological insights, first to wartime problems and later to the exploration of contemporary cultures. In 1953 she returned to Manus to record the dramatic postwar progress of the community she had studied in 1928, described in *New Lives for Old: Cul-*

tural Transformation—Manus, 1928–1953 (1956). In 1965 and 1966 she made further short trips to Manus, and in 1967 she participated in the filming of a ninety-minute color sound film for National Educational Television, "Margaret Mead's New Guinea Journal," showing the gigantic strides into the modern world of a people whom she had known as stone-age children.

For her tireless and imaginative pursuit of knowledge about human potentialities, Margaret Mead has won world-wide recognition both from her colleagues and from the general public. The recipient of many honorary degrees and awards, she was named Outstanding Woman of the Year in the Field of Science by the Associated Press (1949) and one of the outstanding women of the twentieth century by Nationwide Women Editors (1965), and she has received the Omega Award in the field of education (1977). She has been president of the American Anthropological Association (1960), the World Federation for Mental Health (1956–57), the World Society for Ekistics (1969–71), the Society for General Systems Research (1972–73), and the American Association for the Advancement of Science (1975). She has also been a trustee of Hampton Institute in Virginia since 1945.

In June 1969 Margaret Mead became Curator Emeritus of Ethnology at The American Museum of Natural History. She has continued her teaching as Adjunct Professor of Anthropology at Columbia University and Visiting Professor of Anthropology in the Department of Psychiatry at the University of Cincinnati's Medical College. She is also Visiting Professor at the Menninger Foundation in Topeka, Kansas. In addition to her own books and monographs, Dr. Mead has coauthored many books with younger collaborators and writes a monthly column for *Redbook Magazine.*

In her field work, Margaret Mead has been able to follow the children she studied into their adulthood in Manus, Bali, and New Guinea, and in her own lifetime, she, as the grand-daughter, daughter, and mother of professional women, has participated actively in our rapidly changing world.

Books by Margaret Mead

COMING OF AGE IN SAMOA

GROWING UP IN NEW GUINEA

THE CHANGING CULTURE OF AN INDIAN TRIBE

SEX AND TEMPERAMENT IN THREE PRIMITIVE SOCIETIES

FROM THE SOUTH SEAS

AND KEEP YOUR POWDER DRY

BALINESE CHARACTER: A PHOTOGRAPHIC ANALYSIS, with Gregory Bateson

MALE AND FEMALE

GROWTH AND CULTURE: A PHOTOGRAPHIC STUDY OF BALINESE CHILDHOOD, with Frances C. Macgregor

THE SCHOOL IN AMERICAN CULTURE

SOVIET ATTITUDES TOWARD AUTHORITY

NEW LIVES FOR OLD: CULTURAL TRANSFORMATION—MANUS, 1928–1953

AN ANTHROPOLOGIST AT WORK: WRITINGS OF RUTH BENEDICT

PEOPLE AND PLACES

CONTINUITIES IN CULTURAL EVOLUTION

ANTHROPOLOGY: A HUMAN SCIENCE

ANTHROPOLOGISTS AND WHAT THEY DO

FAMILY, with Kenneth Heyman

THE WAGON AND THE STAR: A STUDY OF AMERICAN COMMUNITY INITIATIVE, with Muriel Brown

THE SMALL CONFERENCE: AN INNOVATION IN COMMUNICATION, with Paul Byers

A RAP ON RACE, with James Baldwin

A WAY OF SEEING, with Rhoda Metraux

BLACKBERRY WINTER: MY EARLIER YEARS

RUTH BENEDICT

WORLD ENOUGH: RETHINKING THE FUTURE, with Kenneth Heyman

LETTERS FROM THE FIELD: 1925–1975

Books Edited by Margaret Mead

COOPERATION AND COMPETITION AMONG PRIMITIVE PEOPLES

CULTURAL PATTERNS AND TECHNICAL CHANGE

PRIMITIVE HERITAGE: AN ANTHROPOLOGICAL ANTHOLOGY, with Nicholas Calas

A STUDY OF CULTURE AT A DISTANCE, with Rhoda Metraux

CHILDHOOD IN CONTEMPORARY CULTURES, with Martha Wolfenstein

THE GOLDEN AGE OF AMERICAN ANTHROPOLOGY, with Ruth Bunzel

AMERICAN WOMEN, with Frances B. Kaplan

SCIENCE AND THE CONCEPT OF RACE, with Theodosius Dobzhansky, Ethel Tobach, and Robert E. Light

THE ATMOSPHERE: ENDANGERED AND ENDANGERING, with William Kellogg

Contents

Preface to the Revised Edition   xv

PART I: From the Perspective of the 1960s
ONE: The Task Before Us: The 1960s   3
TWO: Postfigurative Cultures and Well-Known
     Forebears   13
THREE: Cofigurative Cultures and Familiar Peers   39
FOUR: Prefigurative Cultures and Unknown Children   65

PART II: From the Perspective of the 1970s
FIVE: The Domestication of the Generation Gap   95
SIX: Unanticipated Reverberations of the
     Generation Gap   109
SEVEN: New Forms of Commitment   121
EIGHT: Hope Within Technology   133
NINE: Safeguarding Diversity   147

APPENDIX A Bibliographical Note   159
APPENDIX B Films, Slides, and Music Used in the
     Man and Nature Lectures   165
Related Readings   167
Index   171

Preface to the Revised Edition

This book is based on what I have learned about the way human cultures are transmitted and changed, as I have watched primitive cultures come into the modern world during my last fifty years of field work in the Pacific. Since the first edition of this book, I have made three trips to the Pacific, revisiting the Manus, whom I first studied in 1928, and revisited four other groups in various stages of transition. In between I have attended international conferences and discussed issues like food and population, transition and change—problems of the world—with people from many countries. At Columbia University I have taught a great variety of students, and I have lectured to and held discussions with student audiences all over the country and carefully considered their questions.

It is on these experiences that I base my statements. As a cultural anthropologist, I am concerned with the cultural aspects of the generation gap and generational change and their implications for the world community. It was to these concerns that the old pages in the book were addressed, and the new chapters are addressed to them also.

The ideas which underlie this book have been growing as the world has been changing. The ways in which we are able to think about ourselves have been evolving as fast as the new knowledge and the new institutions which surround us. When I read the 1970 edition over carefully, alert to what could stand and what must be changed, to what statements remained an accurate expression of what we now know and which now had an odd archaic ring, I became newly aware not only of how much the world had changed but of how much my own understanding had changed since 1968 when I first prepared to give a series of lectures in the 1969 *Man and Nature* series at The American Museum of Natural History, on which the first edition of this book was based. I always value more the few sentences of measured praise from my own colleagues than more lightly given accolades, so I was pleased to have been asked to give these three lectures. In 1965 Jacob Bronowski gave the first lectures in the series and I had rushed back from Washington, to slip into an evening dress in the dusty, little-used green room of the old auditorium and listen to the enchantment that he imparted to his audience as he let each phrase linger so long that by the end of the lecture, his listeners felt they had known it all along.

But I wanted what I had to say to be sharply realized as new, as Bronowski had wanted what he said to be experienced as universal. We were living through a period, from the first outbreaks in American universities in 1964 to those in Paris in May of 1968 and the "cultural revolution" in China, which made many people think the world had come to an end. Explanations for the state of things abounded: the Vietnam war in the United States, Algeria and De Gaulle in France, the decay of capitalism, the rise of communism, the effects of drugs, the aftermath of World War II which had disinherited a generation in Germany, the rise of affluence, the disappointments of the end of the American civil rights movement's apocalyptic hopes. Periodically, people referred to the "Generation Gap," which was even beginning to appear in the ads on TV: "Gee, Dad, do you dig margarine?" asks the unrepentant, long-haired son shown at a breakfast table. "Yes. Like this," replies the disapproving father, putting a knife into the bowl of margarine!

As I looked at what was happening and at the varied and often incompatible explanations that were being given, I remembered the political ad for the presidential hopeful Eugene McCarthy in the New York *Times* of February, 1968 showing a host of beautiful, eager children. "Your children have come back to you," it said, extending the hope to parents that the Pied Piper had not taken them away for good. And I began to realize that something very new was happening in the world. It was not just *a* generation gap—for we had had many before, between particular groups of old-fashioned parents and modern children, but an event that could be spelled with capital letters, as unique events are— *the* Generation Gap—world-wide, something that had never occurred before simultaneously and on such a scale. There had been many small gaps, between rural parents and urban children; between pioneers in a new country and the children who were born there, listening to the songs of new birds their parents had never heard in childhood; between the comfortable, pre-World War I, complacent world and those who grew up after the lamps of Europe went out, not to be "lit again in our lifetime"; between those reared in communities of unquestioning religious dogma and their children who went away to have every belief challenged. All of these familiar happenings were called up by the phrase "Generation Gap." People somehow felt it was worse than usual; more children were alienated from their parents. For one black sheep in a flock of doubtful future offspring, there seemed suddenly to be the risk of a whole flock—the entire graduating class of a high school.

There were strange things going on that people vaguely sensed as different or set their thoughts so stubbornly against trying to understand that they were immune to ordinary reasonable arguments. In the past, stern prohibitionists had threatened to disinherit their children if they smoked or drank. Puritanical groups, intent upon democratizing religion by making every one abstain from pleasure, had passed laws against the sale of liquor or cigarettes, against gambling or even kissing one's wife on Sunday, and the children shared the fate of the entire population. But in the 1960s and 1970s, we witnessed quite a new phenomenon: parents who were not stern prohibitionists, parents who drank and smoked freely even excessively, not only forbidding their children their preferred indulgences—specifically marijuana—but threatening to kill the children who used it. Nor, said the obsessed parents, would it do the children any good to grow up; never, never would they be allowed to smoke "pot." Where had this new, utter irrationality come from, as threatening parents stood, martini in one hand, cigarette in the other, replying to the analogy between alcohol, nicotine, and *Cannabis sativa,* "I don't see what the martini has to do with it."

On the children's side, there were equally new and superficially inexplicable signs of change; homilies and proclamations from the Establishment were met, not with the slogans of revolution or religious conversion, old ways in which young people had rebelled, but by a shower of obscenities that were as monotonously repellent of adult comments as the electronically amplified music that protected the young against adult presences.

A new search for identity was beginning, identity of many different kinds—as a new American (the term "white ethnic" had not been invented); as a "black" ("black is beautiful" was just becoming a nationwide slogan); as a middle-aged husband sick of the responsibilities of too early marriage and parenthood; as a woman, educated to be a person, trapped in a suburb; as an elderly person, set aside to rot and die on the rubbish heap of a throwaway society.

But while everyone—young, middle-aged, or elderly; black or white; born of European, African, or Asian stock; speaking with the flat accents of the old New Englander or the drawl of the Old South Easterner—was concerned with the search for identity, commitment became a central problem for the young.

I came to see that both the search for identity and the uncertainty about commitment were part of the same larger issue: the way in which the whole world was caught in an unprecedented situation, as young and old—adolescents and all their elders—faced each other across a yawning gap. The French translate the word "gap" in "Generation Gap" as *fosse,* a ditch, which is a far bettter word. "Gap" is vague, lacks concreteness, is subject to all sorts of verbal necromancy, so people can ask, "Is the Generation Gap getting narrower? Is the Generation Gap closing?" But a deep, man-made ditch, dug by human beings who have invented a technology which divided all those reared before the mid-forties from all those who have grown up afterward, cannot close; it cannot narrow. Think of a ditch as deep as the Grand Canyon and parallel with the Pacific Ocean, moving slowly toward the Pacific, with people standing on each side. Each year there will be fewer people on my side of the great Generation Gap—and when it, metaphorically, reaches the Pacific Ocean and the last member of the generation reared before the forties, anywhere in the world, has died, then and only then, will the Generation Gap be a matter of history.

Meanwhile, and especially in the 1960s, when the first of the new generation reached the colleges around the world, both young and old were uniquely isolated. Adults, over thirty or so, had to realize that there would never be people like ourselves again, people reared in a partly explored world, a world in which there was no atomic bomb and so no danger of total destruction, no TV and man-made satellites to send messages around the world in seconds, no possibility of going to the moon, no computers to condense a lifetime of calculations into a few minutes. We, on our side of the Gap, had been born and bred in an age before the second Fall, incapable of destroying the whole human race, and innocent of the terrible responsibility now upon us all. The ancient lure of parenthood, which had kept men and women of the past reproducing and laboring for hundreds of generations, so that others like themselves could live as they had lived, is gone. Our generation, in a curiously final way, will have no successors. None of the new generation will ever appreciate the wonders of space flight as we do, we who never believed it was possible. No one of the new generation will have to pause almost a minute to connect the moon in the sky and the radioed report from an Apollo mission.

The young, standing on the other side of the Gap, face a world without models and without precedent. No one, of all those on whom the young have depended since we became human, is now what they themselves will, or can, become. Neither parents nor teachers, lawyers, doctors, skilled workers, inventors, preachers, or prophets can be models for those who had such a different childhood. As lonely for the young as for the old, the 1960s were unique in human history, for we knew for the first time that what was true of us, in our country, our community, our class, was true for the whole world. We knew that we could no longer fantasize that somewhere on this planet, somewhere in this solar system, there would be other creatures not subject to the same vicissitudes as we are. Everyone was in and counted; the radio waves ringed the world. There were no answers in our solar system.

The student outbreaks around the world occurred when the new generation arrived at the colleges and universities, separated from their preforties parents, able to think, to judge what they saw with fresh eyes, to look at a world that had never existed before; a world into which all young people, no matter how ancient or undeveloped their nations, were entering at once.

That moment was like a great spasm which affected all of us, and I·felt that only if we could understand it would we be able to live through it constructively. The Gap would not narrow, but as the newly enfranchised young got older and their astounded and embittered elders got used to the fact, it would be possible to talk across it; but this would require an understanding of how it had come about.

MARGARET MEAD

The American Museum of Natural History
New York
September 1977

CULTURE AND
COMMITMENT

PART I

From the Perspective
of the 1960s

CHAPTER ONE

The Task Before Us: The 1960s

An essential and extraordinary aspect of our present state [in 1960s] is that, at this moment in which we are approaching a world-wide culture and the possibility of becoming fully aware citizens of the world in the late twentieth century, we have simultaneously available to us for the first time examples of the ways men and women have lived at every period over the last fifty thousand years: primitive hunters and fishermen; people who have only digging sticks to cultivate their meager crops; people living in cities that are still ruled in theocratic and monarchical style; peasants who live as they have lived for a thousand years, encapsulated and walled off from urban cultures; peoples who have lost their ancient and complex cultures to take up simple, crude, proletarian existences in the new; and peoples who have left thousands of years of one kind of culture to enter the modern world, with none of the intervening steps. At the time that a New Guinea native looks at a pile of yams and pronounces them "a lot" because he cannot count them, teams at Cape Kennedy calculate the precise second when an Apollo mission must change its course if it is to orbit around the moon. In Japan, sons in the thirteenth generation of potters who make a special ceremonial pot are still forbidden to touch a potter's wheel or work on other forms of pottery. In some places old women search for herbs and mutter spells to relieve the fears of pregnant girls, while elsewhere research laboratories outline the stages in reproductivity that must each be explored in order to develop better contraceptives. Armies of twenty savage men go into the field to take one

more victim from a people they have fought for five hundred
years, and international assemblies soberly assay the vast destructiveness of nuclear weapons. Some fifty thousand years
of our history lie spread out before us, accessible for this
brief moment in time to our simultaneous inspection.

This is a situation that has never occurred before in human
history and, by its very nature, can never occur in this way
again. It is because the entire planet is accessible to us that
we can know that there are no people anywhere about whom
we might know but do not. One mystery has been resolved
for us forever as it applies to earth, and future explorations
must take place among the planets and the stars. We have
the means of reaching all of earth's diverse peoples and we
have the concepts that make it possible for us to understand
them, and all the earth's peoples now share in a world-wide,
technologically propagated culture, within which they are
able to listen as well as to talk to us. For the one-sided explorations of the early anthropologists who recorded the strange
kinship systems of alien peoples, to whom they themselves
were utterly unintelligible, we now can substitute open-
ended conversations, conducted under shared skies, when
airplanes fly over the most remote mountains, and primitive
people can tune in transistor radios or operate tape recorders
in the most remote parts of the world. The past culture of
complex civilizations is largely inaccessible to the technologically simplest peoples of the world. They know nothing
of three thousand years of Chinese civilization, or of the
great civilizations of the Middle East, or of the traditions of
Greece and Rome from which modern science has grown.
The step from their past to our present is condensed, but
they share one world with us, and their desire for all that
new technology and new forms of organization can bring
now serves as a common basis for communication.

This has happened while many other things have been
happening in the world. The old colonial empires have broken up. Countries with a dozen college graduates have become nations, and peoples newly joined together politically

demand to be heard as nations. The voiceless and the oppressed in every part of the world have begun to demand more power. Fourth-grade children conduct sit-ins and undergraduates claim the right to choose their professors. A profound disturbance is occurring in the relationships between the strong and the weak, the possessors and the dispossessed, the elder and the younger, and those who have knowledge and skill and those who lack them. The secure belief that those who knew had authority over those who did not has been shaken.

Profound as these changes are, I do not think we would have found it easy to bring into our councils the full contribution of members of exotic and primitive cultures, if at the same time a world-wide culture had not been developing.

In 1967, after an absence of twenty-nine years, I returned to the village of Tambunam on the Sepik River in New Guinea. In many ways progress had passed it by. Although a mission had been admitted to the village to provide schooling for children, ceremonies had been constricted, war abolished, and the great men's house removed, these people still built their beautiful dwelling houses, worked sago, and fished as they had always done. Yet there was a difference. In the 1930s, when one arrived in a New Guinea village, the first requests were for medicine, as someone came forward with a festering wound or bad laceration, and for trade goods—razor blades, fishhooks, salt, adze blades, cloth. The European was expected to bring material objects from the outside world and, if he stayed, to make it easier for the village people to obtain these goods. But in 1967 the first conversation went:

"Have you got a tape recorder?"

"Yes, why?"

"We have heard other people's singing on the radio and we want other people to hear ours."

A major shift. Through the spread of a world culture of transistor radios and democratic theories about the value of each small culture, the people of Tambunam had heard New

Guinea music, which it was now Australian-United Nations government policy to broadcast, and they had come to feel that they could participate, on an equal footing, in this new world of broadcasting. This was not all. As my colleague Rhoda Metraux began to record their music, they became skilled critics and producers, learning how to hear the interfering sounds of dogs barking and babies crying—sounds they had never attended to when there was no tape recorder to tell them how much of the repertoire of village sounds was audible and how these sounds spoiled their performance. As they listened to the nondiscriminating, pedantic tape, a new set of self-perceptions was available to them. They now included the direction of the wind as they considered how their music could be recorded best and they learned to modulate the loudness of percussion instruments to match the carrying quality of different singers' voices. The kind of awareness that is the first step in an ability to participate in social science had reached them through a new climate of opinion and a new technology. They shared our world and could contribute to it in a new way.

Today we face a new situation, confronted by what is happening all over the world. In the United States we can visit a Shriners' hospital for burned children and find there the extraordinary beauty and devotion of a whole team of highly trained doctors and nurses who dedicate thousands of hours to the care of badly burned children, patiently regrafting skin and remodeling features to give brave and optimistic children a semblance of what they might have been. Such single-minded devotion to recovery, to remade skin, and to simulated hands, gives one an extraordinary hope for the future. We see, however, that in the same hospital other children, who have no capacity for such optimism and who face with despair the future as deformed and mutilated creatures are still forced to live, ingenuously and lovingly wooed back to life and partial functioning by the same system that saves their optimistic little roommates. When we realize that those who have given money and time and skill to make such miracles possible are citizens, and in most cases not actively dissenting citizens, of a country that was engaged each day in a war in which more children are burned with napalm than such hospitals save in a year, one's heart falters. Are we trapped, one is forced to ask? Are we trapped, not by a set of immutable instincts which determine that we will always, in all cases, turn to aggression and exploitation of others whenever we are strong enough or, to quote an equally persuasive theory, whenever we are too weak? Are we trapped instead within a set of inventions called "civilization" that is now so well supported by technology and population expansion that we must follow a predetermined course to destruction, just as all the earlier civilizations did, but this time on a planetary scale which will end the history of inhabitants of Terra of Sol?

If I believed that this were so, that the greater man's capacity to invent, elaborate, and transmit complex cultures, the more surely he would be trapped in a cultural setting which, while it permitted great achievements, would ultimately lead to destruction and horror, I should not have written this book. The role of a prophet of doom is a useful one only if it is not believed by the prophets themselves. Who will take the trouble to warn of the doom to come unless some preferred future alternative is offered, either in steps that will avert that doom or in preparation for a next world? The more vigorously doomsday is preached, the more one is committed to a better world. It may, however, be the spurious promise that man, having ravished and destroyed earth, will set off for another planet. Or it may be the completely transcendental alternative that the Lord has had enough of us and will allow us to precipitate catastrophes that will permit the chosen to enter heaven and the rejected to burn forever in the fires of hell.

When the causes of great catastrophes were not understood, a conception of a God who purified with fire or flood, but saved some men for a future on earth, was a tenable one, a belief in fact that permitted those who held it to survive through the most terrible vicissitudes. It permitted men to live and pit their strength and optimism against tremendous odds, confident that they, the chosen people, would survive. So men have returned to build again and again on the slopes of volcanoes; in Kansas the residents of each small town that has never had a tornado continue to believe that they, favored above others, will never have one. And in some American communities scientists have joined in the protests of local citizens against the location of dangerous facilities near *their* cities, fully conscious that if their protests were successful the missile site would be built near someone else's city. The physicist Leo Szilard, low in faith in the species of which he was such a distinguished member, proposed a set of target cities in the United States and the U.S.S.R., which would be marked for reciprocal sacrifice, so that the self-interest of each city so marked would prevent nuclear war.

None of these partial views of man as sometimes condemned and sometimes chosen, in either secular or religious form, stands up within our present single, intercommunicating, world-wide settlement pattern. No spurious pattern of promise of escape in space colonization, no doctrine of a God who would destroy the many to save a few, no persistence of blind optimism will suffice. The prophets who fail to present a bearable alternative and yet preach doom are part of the trap that they postulate. Not only do they picture us caught in a tremendous man-made or God-made trap from which there is no escape, but we also must listen to them, day in, day out, describe how the trap is inexorably closing. To such prophecies the human race, as presently bred and educated and situated, is incapable of listening. So some dance and some immolate themselves as human torches; some take drugs and some spill their creativity in sets of randomly placed dots on a white ground. The concerned may be too few to take the steps needed to save us. Unless there are enough such men and women, we are doomed. So I stand here, not as a Cassandra, but as one who lived through the urgencies of World War II, when, under pressure of what seemed inevitable disaster, we as a people were able to rally what resources we had to fend off that disaster. And I now believe that one of the essential elements in escape from an infinitely greater threat is the willingness to use—each one of us—what we know now, always acknowledging that what we know is not enough. Then the urgency was great. We foresaw the death of science and humane culture as we had known them, and the submergence of the Western world by a demonic culture that could not only use the technology developed by science for its own demonic ends, but also prevent science itself from generating liberating humane change. We foresaw a hundred years of "dark ages," and so limited were we, in our conception of time and space, that a hundred years of eclipse of Euro-American culture then seemed too terrible to contemplate. Perhaps it was just because it was thus limited that we could face it. In contrast, the possibility of the disappearance of all human life, of life itself, from this planet is something few human beings can imagine. Using the imagery of theology or science fiction, human beings see all else destroyed but themselves. Theirs is the same fatuous optimism I myself once displayed when the car in which I was being driven swerved toward what seemed certain destruction. Thinking of the children of the driver soon to be orphaned, I said to myself: "I'll take care of them."

Such optimism is both our hope and our greatest danger. Displayed by a single child, who can testify to our increasing concern for the individual, such optimism may illumine the world. Displayed by members of a whole community, who rebuild their houses on the slopes of an active volcano, it may lead to world-wide destruction. A balance between individual optimism and stubborn group blindness is what we seek. Perhaps one of the ways of achieving this balance is to find those who, drawing on their own individual and group history, have an extra capacity for optimism. We can then provide them with the tools of observation and forecasting that will set them looking for new sites and cities, better than the familiar slopes of active volcanoes. This is what I hope.

I believe that the reason we can look at all the great civilizations of the past and at the successive stages in the history of our own era as a succession of repetitive traps is that *we do not know enough about them.* It is upon great historic emptinesses—the lives of unknown peoples lived out within high-standing broken walls now in ruins, the songs sung to infants that we cannot reconstruct, and the lives of the unsung poor and dispossessed who left no records at all—that the human imagination can project its fantasies and its despair. In history, as in science, the grand design without the detail shakes belief and trust to the core. The first understanding of Darwinian theory aroused only anguish in those who trusted their God and justified a dog-eat-dog social theory in those who did not.

Every detailed exploration of the mechanisms of survival—of the delicate adjustments that permit many brightly colored creatures to live crowded together in distinctive niches in the tropical seas and less specialized creatures to move from one habitat to another—modulates the original response of the sensitive to the idea of the "survival of the fittest." For the theory of a death instinct in lemmings, we can substitute a delicate response to conditions of overcrowding or shortage of food.

Each view of the world, in a crude overstatement of theory, has led us into one trap after another as we have seen human society as a sanctioned analogue of nature red in tooth and claw, or the universe as a machine that man can learn to control, or man himself as a machinelike mechanism that can soon be manufactured in large replicated quantities. But the next advances in theory, the use of new instruments, and finer methods of observation and analysis have transformed these crude exploitative ideas and the complementary despair that they arouse in the sensitive into new levels of complexity.

The appropriate activity for human beings is no longer to

be phrased in terms of the crude maximization of a single variable or of a few variables, where loss is balanced by gain and gain inevitably means loss somewhere in the system. Such maximization models are found where crop yield is promoted at the expense of depleting the soil or polluting the streams; or, in the socio-economic sphere, when one country's economic progress is seen as inevitably linked to another country's loss. Instead of the model of the single, isolated organism as a physical unit in a mechanical system, we may use a biological model, especially an ecological model based on a complex system of many living creatures in interaction with a single environment. In this model, the gain of one part is the gain of other parts of the system. Parasite and host are essential to each other; change comes when the internal balance is disturbed and new adjustments have to be made. The old calculus of gain and loss is replaced by negative entropy in which concentrations of information reverse the trend toward disorganization. This is the path human beings have to take if they are both to use and to escape from their previous scientific insights. In this way, through the understanding that they acquire of the universe they live in, human beings, in the universe, come to be exemplars and executants of the highest exercise of negative entropy.

All such changes from crude and inherently pessimistic phrasings and conceptions to those that permit room for innovation, consciousness, and salvation proceed from new and relevant research. The various tools made possible by mathematics, electronics, and technology in general can be used with greater and greater precision to explore events, the scale or composition of which have hitherto been taken for granted or which have been treated as units of the larger system without intrinsic characteristics of their own. Each discovery of a new level of scientific penetration of the nature of the universe which includes human beings opens up new vistas of hope.

But the use of the physical sciences alone, however much they are directed toward the protection of the planet and the cultivation of human values, will not be enough. Only if we use also the age-old methods through which human beings, by exploring themselves, have come to understand their human possibilities better, can we hope to provide a firm basis for commitment and hope.

CHAPTER TWO

Postfigurative Cultures
and Well-Known Forebears

In past studies of the way in which culture is transmitted, I have found it useful to distinguish between those cultures in which change is so slow that it seems as if a child's cultural expectations could be defined at birth and those in which change was more rapid so that some young people and even some adults had to learn from their peers rather than from their elders. We have now entered a new phase, in which adults all over the world have to recognize that all children's experience is different from their own. To distinguish these three cultural styles I am using the words *postfigurative,* when the future repeats the past, *cofigurative,* in which the present is the guide to future expectations, and *prefigurative* for the kind of culture in which the elders have to learn from the children about experiences which they have never had. Primitive societies and small religious and ideological enclaves are primarily postfigurative, deriving authority from the past. Great civilizations, which necessarily have developed techniques for incorporating change, characteristically make use of some form of cofigurative learning from peers, playmates, fellow students, and fellow apprentices. We are now entering a period, new in history, in which the young are taking on new authority in their prefigurative apprehension of the still unknown future.

A postfigurative culture is one in which change is so slow and imperceptible that grandparents, holding newborn grandchildren in their arms, cannot conceive of any other fu-

ture for the children than their own past lives. The past of
the adults is the future of each new generation; their lives
provide the ground plan. The children's future is shaped in
such a way that what has come after childhood for their forebears is what they, too, will experience after they are grown.

Postfigurative cultures, in which the elders cannot conceive
of change and so can only convey to their descendants this
sense of unchanging continuity, have been, on the basis of
present evidence, characteristic of human societies for millennia or up to the beginning of civilization. Without written or
monumental records, each change had to be assimilated to
the known and carried on in the memory and the movement
patterns of the elders of each generation. Children's basic
learning was conveyed so early, so inarticulately, and so
surely, as their elders expressed the sense that this was the
way things would be because children were the children of
their elders' bodies and spirits, their elders' land and tradition, particular and specific, that each child's sense of identity and destiny was unchallengeable. Only the impact of
some violent external event like a natural catastrophe or a
military conquest could alter this. Contact with other peoples
might not change this sense of timelessness at all; the sense
of difference reinforced the sense of one's own particular and
ineradicable identity. Even the extreme conditions of forced
migration, long voyages with no known or certain destination
on uncharted seas and arrival on an uninhabited island, only
accentuated this sense of continuity.

It is true that the continuity of all cultures depends on the
living presence of at least three generations. The essential
characteristic of postfigurative cultures is the assumption, expressed by members of the older generation in their every
act, that their way of life (however many changes may, in
fact, be embodied in it) is unchanging, eternally the same. In
the past, before the present extension of life span, living
great-grandparents were very rare and grandparents were
few. Those who embodied the longest stretch of the culture,
who were the models for those younger than themselves, in

whose slightest tone or gesture acceptance of the whole way of life was contained, were both few and hale. Their keen eyesight, sturdy limbs, and tireless industry represented physical as well as cultural survival. For such a culture to be perpetuated, the old were needed, not only to guide the group to seldom-sought refuges in time of famine but also to provide the complete model of what life was. When the end of life is already known—when the song that will be sung at death, the offerings that will be made, the spot of earth where one's bones will rest are already designated—each person, according to age and sex, intelligence and temperament, embodies the whole culture.

In such cultures, every object, in its form and in the way it is handled, accepted, rejected, misused or broken, or inappropriately venerated, reinforces the way in which every other object is made and used. Each gesture reinforces, recalls, and reflects or provides a mirror image or an echo of each other gesture, of which it is a more complete or less complete version. Each utterance contains forms found in other utterances. Any segment of cultural behavior, when analyzed, will be found to have the same underlying pattern or the same kind of patterned allowances for the existence of other patterns in that culture. The very simple cultures of peoples who have been isolated from other peoples make the point most sharply. But cultures that are very complex may yet be postfigurative in style, and so may display all the characteristics of other postfigurative cultures: the absence of a realization of change and the successful printing, indelibly, upon each child of the cultural form.

The conditions for change are, of course, always present implicitly, even in the mere repetition of a traditional procedure. As no one can step into the same river twice, so there is always a possibility that some procedure, some custom, some belief, acceded to a thousand times, will rise into consciousness. This chance increases when the people of one postfigurative culture are in close contact with those of another. Their sense of what indeed constitutes their culture is accentuated.

In 1925 after a hundred years of contact with modern Euro-American cultures, Samoans talked continually about *Samoa* and *Samoan* custom, rebuking small children as *Samoan* children, combining their remembered Polynesian identity and their sense of the contrast between themselves and the colonizing foreigners. In the 1940s, in Venezuela, within a few miles of the city of Maracaibo, Indians still hunted with bows and arrows, but cooked their food in aluminum pots stolen from Europeans, with whom they had never communicated in any way. And in the 1960s, living as enclaves within a foreign country, European or American troops and their families stationed there have looked with equally uncomprehending and unaccepting eyes at the "natives"—Germans, Malays, or Vietnamese—who lived outside their compounds. The experience of contrast may only heighten the sense of the elements of changeless identity of the group to which one belongs.

While postfigurative cultures are characteristically intimately related to their habitat, the habitat need not be a single area where twenty generations have tilled the same soil. Such cultures are found also among nomadic peoples who move twice a year, among groups in diaspora like the Armenians and the Jews, in Indian castes who live represented by small numbers scattered among villages inhabited by many other castes. They may be found among small groups of aristocrats or among outcastes like the *eta* of Japan. People who were once parts of complex societies may forget—in foreign lands—the kinds of dynamic responses to realized change that caused them to emigrate, and in the new place they may huddle together, again asserting their unchanging identity with their forebears.

Adoption into such groups, conversion, initiation, circumcision—none of these is impossible; but all such acts convey absolute commitment and irrevocability conveyed by grandparents to their own grandchildren in postfigurative cultures.

Membership, normally achieved by birth and sometimes by election, is a matter of total and unquestioning commitment.

The postfigurative culture depends upon the actual presence of three generations. So the postfigurative culture is peculiarly generational. It depends for continuity upon the expectations of the old and upon the almost ineradicable imprint of those expectations upon the young. It depends upon the adults' being able to see the parents who reared them, as they rear their own children in the way they themselves were reared. In such a society there is no room for the invocation of mythical parent figures, who in a changing world are so frequently conjured up to justify parental demands—"My father would never have done this or that or t'other"; such statements cannot be resorted to when a grandfather is sitting there, in comfortable league with his small grandson, while the father himself is the opponent of both, because of the discipline that exists between father and son. The whole system is there; it depends upon no version of the past which is not also shared by those who have heard that version since they were born and who therefore experience it as actuality. The answers to the questions "Who am I? What is the nature of my life as a member of my culture? How do I speak and move, eat and sleep, make love, making a living, become a parent, meet my death?" are experienced as predetermined. It is possible for children to fail to be as brave or as parental, as industrious or as generous, as the dictates which their grandparents' hands conveyed to them, but in their failure, they are as much members of their culture as others are in their success. If suicide is a known possibility, a few or many may commit suicide; if is not, the self-destructive impulses take other forms. The combination of universal human drives and available human defense mechanisms, the processes of recognition and apperception, of recognition and recall, of redintegration, will be there. But the style in which these are combined will be overridingly particular and distinctive.

The diverse peoples of the Pacific whom I have been studying for forty years illustrate many kinds of postfigurative

cultures. The Mountain Arapesh of New Guinea, as they
were living in 1932, displayed one form. In the sureness and
the certainty with which each act was performed—the way
the toes were used to pick up something from the ground or
the leaves for the mat were bitten off—each act, each gesture
was adapted to all others in ways that reflected the past, a
past that, however many changes it contained, was itself lost.
For the Arapesh there was no past except the past that had
been embodied in the old and, in a younger form, in their
children and their children's children. Change there had
been, but it had been so completely assimilated that
differences between earlier and later acquired customs had
vanished in the understanding and the expectations of the
people.

As the Arapesh child was fed, held, bathed, and or-
namented, a myriad of inexplicit and inarticulate learnings
were conveyed to it by the hands that held it, the voices
around it, the cadences of lullaby and dirge. Within the village and between villages, as the child was carried over and
later walked on expected paths, the slightest disturbance of
the surface was an event to be registered in the walking feet.
When a new house was built, the response of each person
who passed it registered for the carried child that there was
something new here, something that had not been here a few
days before and yet was in no way startling or surprising.
The response was as slight as that of the blind to the
different feel of sunlight sifted through trees with different
kinds of leaves, yet it was there. The appearance of strangers
in the village was registered with equal precision. Muscles
tensed as people ran over in their minds how much food they
had on hand to placate the dangerous visitors and the proba-
ble whereabouts of their own men who were away from the
village. When a new baby was being born over the edge of
the cliff, in the "evil place" where menstruating and par-
turient women were sent, the place of menstruation, defeca-
tion, and birth, a thousand small familiar signs proclaimed it,
although no town crier announced what was happening.

Living as the Arapesh believed they had always lived, with
the only past an age of fable, a timeless time away, in a place
where every rock and tree served to restate and reaffirm that
changeless past, the old, the middle-aged, and the young received and conveyed the same set of messages: that this is
what it is to be human, to be a boy or a girl, to be a first-
born or a last-born child, to be born into the clan of the eld-
est brother or the clan of a younger ancestor; that this is
what it is to belong to the half of the village for whom the
hawk is the patron bird and to be someone who will grow up
to speak lengthily at feasts or, if one is born or adopted into
the other side of the village, to grow up as a cockatoo and to
speak briefly. Equally, the child learned that many would not
live to grow up. He or she learned that life is a fragile thing
that may be withheld from the newborn of unwanted sex,
may flicker out in the arms of a nursing mother who loses her
milk when her child cannot flourish on it, may be lost because a kinsman has been angered and has stolen some of
one's body substance and given it to enemy sorcerers. The
child learned, too, that the hold of people on the land around
them was slight and tenuous; that there were deserted villages without people to live in them beneath the trees; that
there were names of yams for which the seed or the charms
to grow them had been lost and only the names remained.
Loss of this kind was not treated as a change, but rather as a
recurrent and expected state in a world, where all knowledge
was fleeting and all valued objects were made by other people and must be imported from them. The dance that was
imported twenty years ago had now been passed on to a
more inland village, and only the anthropologist standing
outside the system or occasionally a member of a neighboring
group, convinced of the inferiority of the mountain people
and looking for a way to illustrate it, might comment on the
parts of the dance they had kept and those they had lost.

The sense of timelessness and all-prevailing custom that I
found among the Arapesh, with its slight overtones of despair
and a fear that knowledge might be lost for good and that

human beings who seemed smaller each generation might indeed disappear, was the more striking because they did not live, as the inhabitants of isolated islands do, cut off from all other peoples. Their villages stretched across a mountain range from the beach to the plains. They traded with and traveled among and entertained peoples who spoke other languages and practiced other but similar customs. This sense of identity between the known past and the expected future is the more striking where small changes and exchanges occur all the time. It is the more striking in an area where so much can be exchanged—pots and bags, spears and bows and arrows, songs and dances, seeds and charms. Women did run away from one tribe to another. There were always one or two strange women living in the village who had to learn to speak the language of the men who claimed them as wives when they came and hid in the menstrual huts. This, too, was part of life, and the children learned that other women later would run away. Boys learned that someday their wives might run away; girls learned that they themselves might run away and have to learn different customs and a different language. This, too, was part of an unchanging world.

Other Pacific islanders, the Polynesians, scattered on remote islands many hundreds of miles apart, settled where some small group had made a landfall after weeks at sea, stripped of part of their possessions forever and with many dead, still were able to re-establish their traditional culture and add a special element to it—the determination to preserve it, firmly anchored by genealogy and mythological authenticating parentage in the past. In contrast, the peoples of New Guinea and Melanesia, dispersing during many more thousands of years over small distances, within diversified habitats, have cherished and accentuated small differences, insisting that a few changes in vocabulary, a change of pace, or a shift in consonants meant a new dialect, and have maintained their sense of changeless identity within a framework of continuous interchange and small, noncumulative diversifications of custom.

We find postfigurative cultures surviving or reconstituted among peoples who have lived through tremendous and, in some fashion, remembered historical changes. The people of Bali have been subjected, over many hundreds of years, to profound foreign influences, from China, from Hinduism, from Buddhism, from another and later form of Hinduism brought by the invading Javanese who were fleeing from Islamic conquerors. In the 1930s, in Bali, the ancient and the modern existed side by side in Balinese sculpture and dances, in the Chinese coins used for currency, in the western acrobatic dances imported from Malaya, and in the bicycles of the ice-cream vendors and the ice containers strapped to their handle bars. Outsiders and the occasional educated Balinese could discern the influence of the high cultures of the East and West, sort out the elements of ritual that belonged to different periods of religious influence, and point out the differences between the Brahmans who followed the Hindu Shivistic rites and those who were Buddhist in origin. The unsophisticated keeper of a low-caste temple in a Balinese village could do this too; he would shift the names he habitually called the village gods from such simple and proper appellations as Betara Desa, god of the village, to the name of a Hindu high god when a high-caste visitor was present. Each village had its individual style, its temples, its trances, and its dances; villages dominated by one high-caste group differed from others dominated by another high caste. Yet two firmly held ideas pervaded Bali that the people reiterated in endless, tireless succession: "Every Balinese village is different"; and "All of Bali is the same." Although they had ways of recording the passing of the years and occasionally monuments were dated, the calendar they lived by was one of cycling days and weeks, with celebrations marking the recurrent coincidence of certain combinations of days. A new palm-leaf book, when a copy was finished—for new books were copies of other books made long ago—was dated by the day and week, but not by the year. Changes, which in Melanesia would differentiate a people from their neighbors, which in Polynesia would be denied and reduced, and which in a culture devoted to the idea of change and progress would be treated as genuine innovations—such changes were treated in Bali simply as changing fashions within a recurrent and essentially unchanging world into which individuals were reborn within their own families, to have a fortunate or an unfortunate life.

The Balinese have a long, rich, highly diversified history of diffusion, immigration, and trade, and yet Balinese culture, as certainly as that of the primitive Arapesh, remained a postfigurative culture until World War II. The rituals of life and death and marriage repeated the same themes. The ritual drama depicting the struggle between the dragon, who represented life and ritual, and the witch, who represented death and fear, was enacted as mothers played age-old teasing games with the children they held in their arms. The witch carried the cloth in which a mother held her baby; the dragon, stripped of his fiery tongue, which dragons usually wear, sheltered his followers within his harmless jaws as he enacted the playful Balinese father's role. There was no break between the experience of the old and the experience of the young. No expectation of change or difference reached the child as it relaxed or tensed with fear and delight in the arms of its mother, who relived her earlier experience in the arms of her own mother, as she watched the witch with her magic cloth throw her attackers, supine, into a trance.

This quality of timelessness is found even among peoples whose ancestors belonged to great civilizations whose members were fully conscious of the possibilities of change. Some immigrants from Europe to North America, especially those who shared a cult belief, settled in the New World and purposefully established communities which re-established the same sense of timelessness and of inescapable identity from one generation to another. Hutterites, Amish, Dunkards, Sikhs, Dukhobors all display these qualities. Even today, in such communities, the children are reared so that the life of the parents and grandparents postfigures the course of their own lives. So reared, it is almost impossible to break away; a break means, inwardly as well as outwardly, such a change in the sense of identity and continuity that it is like a rebirth—rebirth into a new culture.

Under the pressure of contact with cultures which are not postfigurative or are both postfigurative and missionizing, making absorption a part of their own cultural identity, individuals may leave their own culture and enter another. They bring with them the sense of what cultural identity is and the expectation that in the new culture they will strive for identity just as they did in the old. In many instances they merely assign parallel meanings, speaking the new language with the syntax of the old, treating dwellings as interchangeable but decorating or entering the house in the new society as they would have done in the old. This is one of the familiar types of adjustment made by adult immigrants from a postfigurative culture when they enter a strange society. Their internal integration does not change; it is so firm that a great number of mere substitutions of items can be made without loss of identity. Then there comes a time for many adult immigrants when there will be such an accumulation of such interchanged items that the personality can be said to be transformed.

It is not yet known whether this kind of transformation is possible for persons coming from a culture without some concept of transformation. Japanese who were born in the United States but who had been sent home for a long period of education in Japan and then had returned to the United States (those Japanese who were called *kibei* in the difficult days of World War II) had little conflict about loyalty when the moment of choice came. They had learned that one must be loyal, but also that membership in a society can be lost and that allegiance can be changed. The fact they had been loyal and acknowledged Japanese meant that they were able to become loyal Americans. Their postfigurative indoctrination already contained the possibility of complete transfer to another society.

It is by some such process that we may understand what must have been, in primitive times, the life of California Indian women who, because of proliferating incest rules, could not marry within communities in which their own language was spoken and who had to go, as strangers, to live out their whole lives within another language group. Here they developed, over uncounted centuries, a woman's language and a man's language—within the same group. The expectation of contrast between the language and associated culture of one's mother and father became a part of the culture into which one was born, postfigured in the songs a grandmother sang and in women's conversation when they were alone. The newcomer to a tribe had learned from her mother and grandmother that women spoke a different language from men, and the man she married had learned to hear the women's language and to speak the men's. These expectations became part of the supporting expectations of the whole set of intermarrying but linguistically diversified peoples.

Just as postfigurative cultures may contain within them expectations of leaving and entering another culture, so also they may contain types of learning that make any such accommodation impossible. Ishi, the lone California Indian who was found in 1911 waiting for death as the sole survivor of a tribe which had been hunted to death by white men, possessed no previous learning that could give him a full place in the white man's world. The identity he maintained was that of a Yana Indian, demonstrating to eager young anthropology students at the University of California how arrowheads were made by the Yana. His early education and his searing, traumatic experience of ten years of hiding from predatory white men contained no provision for change of his own group membership.

Richard Gould has recently studied desert-dwelling Australian aborigines who had been brought long miles from their own "country," where every bit of their part of the desert was known and invested with deep meaning, to a settlement station where more acculturated aborigines lived. The desert people initiated the method that Australian aborigines had used for countless generations to relate to the other tribes near them—they tried to fit their marriage system together with that of the more acculturated people. But the more acculturated aborigines, those who were partly losing their identity, who no longer hunted and made no sacred ceremonies but who, like their forebears, in the end seemed to resist acculturation, were wary of reciprocation. They showed the scars of past failure to come to real terms with the white man's culture. Australian aborigines had had no objection to a man from another tribe cohabiting with their women, providing that he observed the taboos which defined the marriage classes. But white men had no marriage classes; they had, instead, a deep sense of their own racial superiority. That the aboriginal women were sexually available was a sign to the white men of the indelible inferiority of the aborigines. In contact with white men, the aborigines lost their intricate and well-tried way of interdigitating their particular culture system with that of others, and the resulting paralysis halted acculturation.

The way in which children learn languages from their elders defines how, as adults, they themselves will be able to learn new languages. They may learn each new language as a comparable system which makes transformations possible, as New Guinea peoples surrounded by groups speaking other languages do, as Jews and Armenians have done. Or they may learn their own language as a uniquely correct system, of which all other systems are merely imperfect translations, as young Americans have learned American English when they have been taught by teachers who have rejected the mother tongue of their elders.

So through the ages, children have been brought up in culturally evolved ways into which most but not all the children born within the society can be fitted. Distinctions are made among children in terms of observed individual differences and these are treated as categories into which all children must somehow be fitted. The Balinese distinguish between children who are naturally naughty and those who are naturally sober and virtuous. Very early in a Balinese child's life the decision is made as to which type he or she is; the attribution, whether it fits well or poorly, lasts through old age. The Samoans, like the French, make distinctions based on age, on the point at which children attain a capacity to understand what goes on in their society. But no recorded cultural system has ever had enough different expectations to match all the children who were born within it. Sometimes the child who departs too far from expectations dies. Sometimes it is only stunted and angry or forced into an identification with the opposite sex; such children in turn may grow up to distort the responses of those around them. Neuroses, if we see them as failures of the expected system of upbringing, occur in all known societies.

In all systems of upbringing, some provision has to be made for handling the conflict between the child's springing sexuality and its tiny size, its subordinate position, and its lack of maturity. Sometimes the cultural forms almost match part of the child's precocity, as in fishing and hunting societies, where small boys of five or six can learn their parents' subsistence skills and can marry as soon as they reach puberty. Sometimes extraordinary courage is demanded of very small boys, as for example, among the Mundugumor of New Guinea, who sent children as hostages to a temporarily allied tribe. The children were instructed to learn as much as they could while they were hostages, so that sometime later they could guide a head-hunting raid into the same village. In more complex societies, however, in which adult roles are far beyond the reach of six- and seven-year-olds or even sixteen-year-olds, other methods have to be adopted to reconcile the children to the postponement of maturity. Parents have to defend themselves against a rearousal of their own long suppressed early childhood sexuality. This may become a focus of indulgence, as when little Balinese boys are permitted to wander about in groups, unkempt and unwashed and undisciplined, or when Bathonga small boys are sent to be reared by their mothers' brothers instead of by their stern fathers, or when Zuñi parents themselves avoid conflicts with their children by combining seeming indulgence with secret invitations to the "scare dancers" to come and beat the naughty children.

So in every postfigurative society the reappearance in every generation of the little boy's oedipal challenge to male authority, which may have had biological efficacy in earlier hominid forms, but in all known cultures is inappropriate in children too young for reproduction and responsibility, has to be met if the society is to survive. Children must not be treated in ways that exploit their premature sexual responsiveness, so everywhere there are rules against incest. At the same time, adults must be protected from the memories, fears, hostilities, and desperations that are reactivated in themselves by their children and that may otherwise result in rejection and destruction of the children.

Every social system may also be expected to produce some felicitious exceptions—children to whom event after event conveys a sense of special blessing and good fortune or of special election for deeds greater than those expected of their fellows. These may be institutionalized, as among American Indians, in those cultures in which adolescents and adults sought visions and men with compelling visions became leaders. This allowance for the occurrence of genius—that special combination of gifts of temperament, native endowment, and environmental emphasis—means that when the times are also ripe in ideas, individuals may be able to create new cultural forms by a vision—or a dream. The match between ability and felicity of experience is a function of the culture itself. In a culture in which ideas of invention and change are both lacking, a very specially gifted individual may be needed to introduce even a very minor change, such as a small change in the existing art style, in the use of a new raw material, or in the enlargement of the size of a war party. Such minute changes may require as great gifts as did the discoveries of a Galileo or a Newton, who worked within

the context of a great tradition of scientific growth in knowledge.

We still know very little about how such felicitous breaks
in the system of obtaining conformity and replication occur.
We do not know how it is that some children keep their
spontaneity within systems that dull and discipline spontaneity, how some children learn to keep on wondering after
all the accepted answers have been given or how they remain
extravagantly hopeful in the face of routine conditions of
hunger and despair. During the last half century we have
learned a great deal about trauma, about the exposure of infants or children to events that they are unable or unprepared to bear, but we still know very little about those who
are unusually blessed. This is one of the sets of conditions
about which young people are asking questions.

Intergenerational relationships within a postfigurative society are not necessarily smooth. In some societies each generation is expected to rebel—to flout the expressed wishes of the
old men and to take over power from the generation above
them. Childhood may be experienced as agonizing, and small
boys may live in fear of being seized by elderly uncles and
aunts who perform terrifying ceremonies in their honor. But
when the same small boys are grown, they expect their
brothers and sisters to carry out on behalf of their children
the same ceremonial behavior that had so terrified or
mortified them. In fact, some of the most stable postfigurative
cultures, such as those of the Australian aborigines or the
Banaro of the Keram River in New Guinea, are characteristic
of societies in which the whole population is involved in a ritual of torture and initiation or of differential wife sharing
and sexual initiation, many facets of which can best be described as torture, arousing shame and terror in the recipients.

Just as the prisoner who has slept on a hard bed for many
years dreams of a soft bed but finds, when he comes out of
prison, that he can sleep only on a hard one, and as ill-fed
people who move to a place where better food is found may

still cling to the less nutritive and originally unappealing diets of their childhood, so also human beings seem to hold on more tenaciously to a cultural identity that is learned through suffering than to one that has been acquired through pleasure and delight. Children who have grown up happily in comfortable homes can be more secure and adaptable under new circumstances than those whose early lessons have been painful and frightening. The sense of cultural identity that is drilled in with punishment and threats of total rejection is curiously persistent. A sense of national identity which is defined by suffering and the capacity to suffer, by pride in the earlier heroic suffering of one's ancestors, can be maintained in exile under circumstances that might be expected to dissipate it. A few tremendously durable communities, such as those of the Jews and the Armenians, have displayed a persistent sense of national identity through hundreds of years of persecution and exile.

But the prototype postfigurative culture is the isolated primitive culture, the culture in which only the accommodating memories of its members are there to preserve the story of the past. Among preliterate peoples there are no books to lie quietly on the shelf to give the lie to some revision of past history. The voiceless stones, even when they are carved and shaped by the hands of men, can easily be fitted into a revised version of how the world has always been. Genealogists, unembarrassed by documents, condense history, so that the mythological and the recent past flow together. "That Julius Caesar! He had every man in this village out working on the roads!"

"In the beginning was the void." To destroy the memory of the past or preserve it in a form that merely reinforces the different present has been a continuous and highly functional adjustment by primitive peoples, even those who have been most historically minded, as they have come to believe that their small group originated in the place where they now live.

It is on their knowledge of societies of this kind that anthropologists have drawn in developing the concept of culture. The apparent stability and sense of changeless continuity characteristic of such cultures is built into the model of "a culture" that anthropologists have presented to others, not to anthropologists themselves, who wish to use anthropological concepts in the interpretation of human behavior. But there has always been an apparent contradiction between the way anthropologists have described small, primitive, homogeneous, slowly changing societies and the diversity existing among primitive tribes inhabiting such regions as New Guinea and California. It is obvious that over time great changes, although within approximately the same technological level, must have occurred. Peoples separated, languages diverged. Peoples speaking the same languages have been found hundreds of miles apart; groups with strongly contrasting physical types have been found speaking the same language or sharing the same culture.

What has not been emphasized enough, I believe, is that when there is no written language, no documentation of the past, the perception of the new is rapidly engulfed by the style of the old. The elders who edit the version of the culture that is passed on to the young mythologize or deny change. A people who have lived for only three or four generations in tepees on the great American plains, who have borrowed the tepee style from other tribes, may tell how their ancestors learned to make a tepee by imitating the shape of a curled leaf. In Samoa the elders listened politely to a description of the long voyages of Polynesian ancestors by Te Rangi Hiroa, a Polynesian visitor from New Zealand, whose people had preserved a sacrosanct list of the early voyages which was memorized by each generation. His hosts then replied firmly, "Very interesting, but the *Samoans* originated here in Fitiuta." The visitor, himself half-Polynesian and half-European, and a highly educated man, finally took refuge, in great irritation, in asking them whether or not they were now Christians and believed in the Garden of Eden!

In blurring change and assimilating innovation into a distant past, the reliability of memory in relation to the known plays an important part. We have found that a people who can describe every detail of an event that occurred in a period of relative stability will give much more contradictory and imperfect accounts of events that occurred more recently during a period of greater instability. Events that have to be fitted into an unfamiliar setting take on an air of unreality, and in time, if they are remembered at all, they are fitted again into familiar forms and the details of change, like the process of change, are forgotten. Continuity is maintained by the suppression of memories that disturb the sense of continuity and identity.

Even in cultures in which the idea of change has been incorporated, the use of detail to flesh out the memory of events, whether they are distant or recent in time, serves to preserve a sense of continuity over very long periods. Although this is a technique that may be lost together with the attitudes toward identity and continuity to which it is related, it can also be regained. The persistent, unquestioning sense of identity and of the pervasive rightness of each known aspect of life, characteristic of postfigurative cultures, can occur—and can be reconstituted—at every level of cultural complexity.

Immigrants, coming to new continents like North America or Australia from countries in which literacy is thousands of years old and every ancient town is graced by buildings that proclaim a historical sequence of change, may lose the very idea of change. Without the old records and the old landmarks—the market place, the tree or the mountain around which history clustered—the past is condensed. The style of living in the new country, in which much of the past is preserved, is itself relevant. The fact that people go on speaking the old language and follow some of the old occupations—planting grapes in similar soil, sowing wheat in comparable fields, building houses that retain the old proportions—and that the landscape and even the night, in which the Big Dipper wheels across the same northern sky, are familiar, all this can give the immigrant community a sense of unbroken continuity. And this may persist as long as people live together in a group where the grandparents are still regarded as authorities and their recipes for the care of crops or the preservation of food and the proper handling of adversity are adhered to. In the Scandinavian communities of northern Minnesota, people who had come so far to continue a way of life, preserved a great deal of their culture.

The childhood culture may have been learned so unquestioningly and contact with members of other cultures may have been so slight, so hostile, or so contrasting that the individual's deep sense of who he is may be almost unalterable. There single individuals may live for many years among strangers, working, eating, and sometimes even marrying and rearing children, without questioning their identity or seeking to take on the new identity which, reciprocally, is not offered to them. Or whole groups may establish habits of limited migration, as in Greece or China. All the men may go away to sea when they are grown or they may go to work in the mines, the vineyards, or the factories of another country, leaving their women and children at home. Through the generations, new adaptations are made to the absence of the fathers, but the culture, although altered, can still be transmitted coherently.

But the possibilities of change are much greater when the group is transplanted to another environment in circumstances in which all three generations leave their homeland and move together to a place where the new landscape can be compared to the old—where rivers run or the sea pounds with the same sounds—and much of the old way of life has been preserved, so that the grandparents' memories and the children's experience flow together. The fact that in the new country it is already cold in early September where once one could sit in the sun until October, that there are no sunflower seeds for little cakes, that the berries gathered in the early summer are black instead of red, and that the nuts gathered in autumn have a different shape though they are called by the old name—all these variations introduce a new element into the grandparents' comments: "In the old country" it was different.

This awareness of difference opens the way to a new choice for the children. They can listen and absorb the sense of there and here as being different places, making the fact of migration and change part of their consciousness. In so doing, they may cherish the contrast and look with affection on the few mementos of a previous, different existence; or they may find these ancestral memories burdensome or unalluring and reject them altogether. The government of the new country may insist that immigrants accept a new ideology, give up the living habits of the past, vaccinate their babies, pay taxes, send their young men into the armed service and their children to school to learn the state language. Even without such insistence there are other pressures against listening to the old. If the tales the old tell are too nostalgic—if they speak of the many-storied houses in which they once lived, as the Yemenite Jews did when they were brought to Israel; or romanticize the old snug peasant houses, as the Irish, trapped in city tenements, did—then the stories of the grandparents breed discontent. Past grandeur is poor fare for an empty pot and does little to keep the wind from whistling through the chinks.

So it is not surprising that many peoples, even when they are living together, in their own community, in the land to which they have migrated, exclude from their narrowed lives much of the richness of their premigration past. People who once shared that past, although meagerly, as peasants or proletarians let the echoes of past literacy and history die and settle down to live an attenuated life where they now are. This was the kind of life lived by English-speaking mountain people in parts of the American Southeast. Their culture unmistakably derived many generations before from the British Isles. But groups of people were found, at the outbreak of World War I, who had never left their Appalachian valleys, knew nothing of the nation in which they were living—not

even the name of the nearest large town. Yet once they had
been part of a tradition in which the struggles of kings and
barons had been significant and people had migrated to the
New World for religious and political reasons.

Such attenuations of an older culture, appropriate to a
different habitat, a different form of livelihood, or a different-
sized population, occur all over the world. There are South
American Indians who know how to spin, but who spin only
a kind of string to ornament their bodies and do not weave.
There are peoples among whom kinship has proliferated into
the only form of social organization, whose ancestors were
members of organized empires. There are peoples like the
Mayans and the Cretans whose ways of life even in the same
habitat have become fragmented and who have lost much
that was once intrinsic to their ancestors' cultures.

All such changes alter the quality of the culture. We may,
I think, make useful distinctions as to the nature of change
and the point at which a break comes—the point at which
one must cease to speak of a postfigurative culture and treat
what now exists as a culture of a different type. The only essential and defining characteristic of a postfigurative culture,
or of those aspects of a culture that remain postfigurative in
the midst of great changes in language and in allegiance, is
that a group of people consisting of at least three generations
take the culture for granted, so that the children, as they
grow, accept unquestioningly whatever is unquestioned by
those around them. In such circumstances the amount of culturally patterned and internally consistent behavior that is
learned is enormous and only a very small part of it is made
conscious: the cakes at Christmas are named and commented
upon, but the amount of salt in the potatoes goes unremarked. The painted magical circles on the barns to keep the
milk from souring are named, but the proportions of the
haymow and the milkshed are not mentioned. The prefer-
ential treatment given men and certain animals, the nuances
of relationships between men and women, habits of rising

and going to bed, the ways money is saved and spent, responses to pleasure and pain—these are all great bodies of
transmitted behavior, which, when analyzed, can be shown
to be consistent and omnipresent, but they remain below the
surface of consciousness. It is this unlabeled, unverbalized,
and nonconscious quality that gives to the postfigurative culture, and to the postfigurative aspects of all cultures, great
stability.

The situation of those who learn a new culture in adulthood may also have a large amount of postfigurative-style
learning. No one actually teaches the immigrant from another country how to walk. But as a woman buys the clothes
of her new country and learns to put them on—slips at first
uncomfortably into clothes worn by the women she sees on
the street and then accommodates herself to a dress style in
which she must put the dress on over her head instead of
stepping into it—she begins to acquire the posture and
stance of women in the new culture. Other women respond
to this also unconsciously; they begin to treat the newcomer
more as an insider, less as a stranger, take her into their bed-
rooms and into their confidence. As men put on the strange
new clothes, they learn when they can and when they cannot
stand with their hands in their pockets without arousing comment or causing offense. The process is cumulative and, in
many ways, as apparently effortless and unconscious as the
process through which children learn whatever, in their culture, is not made the subject of special discipline and comment. The people among whom a stranger takes up residence
question their own habitual behavior as little as do the elders
who have lived all their lives within a single culture.

These two conditions, lack of questioning and lack of consciousness, are the key conditions for the maintenance of a
postfigurative culture. The frequency with which the postfigurative style has been re-established after periods of
self-conscious turmoil and revolt suggests that this is a form
that remains as available to us as it once was to our forebears

thousands of years ago. All the discrepancies that lie exposed in the paraphernalia of script and history, archives and coded law, can be reabsorbed into systems that, since they are unquestioned and below the surface of consciousness, are also unassailable by analysis.

The closer such unanalyzed cultural behaviors are to those of the observer, the harder they are to discern, even by the practiced and highly trained observer. In World War II there was relatively small resistance, except among observers who had been using different styles of observation (the "old China hands," as they were called), to cultural analyses of Japan, China, Burma, or Thailand. But the same intellectuals, who were willing to accept analyses of Asian peoples or African peoples, objected strenuously and emotionally when cultural analysis was applied to European cultures that contained many unanalyzed elements that were similar to their own. In these circumstances the defenses against self-analysis that permit a member of any one Euro-American culture to think of himself as a freely acting, culturally unconstrained individual were raised against the analysis of a related—for example, German, Russian, or English—cultural character.

Appropriately, also, the sudden recognition of a specific form of postfiguratively established cultural behavior, when it occurs within one's own setting among people of one's own educational level, is especially illuminating. The unanalyzed belief that other people who look very different physically or live at a very different social level from oneself are somehow different also in deeply hereditary ways is a very persistent one, however strongly people may declare their allegiance to the scientific statement that behaviors associated with race and class are learned, not carried in the genes. Whenever the range of consistent difference is great, people will resort to the genetic explanation. Most people feel that others who are very different from themselves must indeed have inherited such differences. So the understanding of cultural differences becomes most real when individuals can finally accept a cultural explanation of inexplicable elements in the behavior of a French or German colleague whose physique is the same as their own.

It is just these deep, unanalyzed, unarticulated consistencies that are learned from unquestioning elders or unquestioning members of a culture into which they have newly moved, that must be made available to analysis if an understanding of culture is to become both a part of the intellectual apparatus of the human sciences and part of the climate of opinion in which the human sciences can flourish. As soon as human beings knew that they were speaking a language different from the language spoken by their neighbors that was learned by children and could be learned by strangers, they became able to learn second and third languages, to make grammars, to alter their own languages consciously. Language, in this respect, is simply the aspect of culture that has been recognized longest as separable from a human being's heredity. The task of understanding the whole of another culture, the deepest organization of the emotions, the least perceptible differences in posture and gesture, is not a different one from that of understanding another language. But the task of analyzing a whole requires different tools— the implementation of the gifted analytic eye and ear by camera, tape recorder, and instruments of analysis.

Today we have, spread out before us, examples of the various forms of postfigurative cultures, of peoples who represent successive phases of cultural history from hunting and gathering to the present. We have the concepts and the instrumentation with which to study them. And although primitive peoples, inarticulate peasants, and the deprived people of rural backwaters and urban slums cannot tell us directly all that they see and hear, we can record their behavior for later analysis, and we can also put into their own hands cameras so that they can record and so help us see what we, by virtue of our upbringing, cannot see directly. Our knowable past lies open before us to inform us. After a millennium of postfigurative and of cofigurative culture, during which human beings learned old things from their parents and new things from their peers, we have arrived at a new stage in the evolution of human cultures.

CHAPTER THREE

Cofigurative Cultures and Familiar Peers

A cofigurative culture is one in which the prevailing model for members of the society is the behavior of their contemporaries. However, there are few societies in which cofiguration has become the only form of cultural transmission and none is known in which this model alone has been preserved through generations. In a society in which the only model is cofigurative, old and young alike come to assume that it is "natural" for the behavior of each new generation to differ from that of the preceding generation.

In all cofigurative cultures the elders are still dominant in the sense that they set the style and define the limits within which cofiguration is expressed in the behavior of the young. There are societies in which approbation by the elders is decisive for the acceptance of new behavior; that is, the young look not to their peers, but to their elders, for the final approval of change. But at the same time, where there is a shared expectation that members of a generation will model their behavior on that of their contemporaries, especially their adolescent age mates, and that their behavior will differ from that of their parents and grandparents, each individual, as he or she successfully embodies a new style, becomes to some extent a model for others of his or her own generation.

Cofiguration has its beginning in a break in the postfigurative system. Such a break may come about in many ways: through a catastrophe in which a whole population, but particularly the old who were essential to leadership, is decimated; as a result of the development of new forms of technology in which the old are not expert; following migration to a new land where the elders are, and always will be, regarded as immigrants and strangers; in the aftermath of a military conquest in which subject populations are required to learn the language and ways of the conqueror; as a result of religious conversion, when adult converts try to bring up children to embody new ideals they themselves never experienced as children and adolescents; or as a purposeful step in a revolution that establishes itself through the introduction of new and different life styles for the young.

The conditions for change to a cofigurative type of culture became increasingly prevalent after the development of high civilization as access to greater resources made it possible for the members of one society to annex, subjugate, incorporate, enslave, or convert members of other societies and to control or direct the behavior of the younger generation. Often, however, cofiguration, as a style, lasts only for a short period. In situations in which the cultural style of the dominant group is essentially postfigurative, second-generation members of a newly added group (whose parents had no certain models except their peers) may be completely absorbed into a different but still wholly postfigurative culture, as are Israeli-born children in a kibbutz.

Nevertheless, the idea that it is possible to incorporate in a society a very large number of adults differently reared and with different expectations introduces a significant change into the culture of that society. Behavior is no longer so firmly associated with birthright membership in the society that it appears to be essentially inherited, rather than learned. Moreover, as the new groups which have been absorbed in the older population still maintain some parts of their own culture, it is possible to distinguish between the children of birthright members and the children of the newly absorbed. The idea that large numbers of individuals of different ages can be assimilated may produce a new flexibility and tolerance of difference. But it may also stimulate the development of countermeasures, such as a firmer drawing of caste lines to ensure that the newcomers will be prevented from attaining the privileges of birthright members.

So it is useful to compare different kinds of cultural absorption. Where absorption took the form of slavery, as a rule, large groups of adults were forcibly removed from their own homeland. They were denied the right to follow most of their own customs and their behavior was regulated by those who enslaved them. Primitive African societies practiced slavery on a large scale. Enslavement was used as a punitive measure within the society; but even slaves coming from other groups were culturally and physically similar to those who enslaved them. In many cases the slaves had rights that could not be denied them. And within a relatively short period the families and descendants of the enslaved were absorbed into the free society. The stigmata of slavery remained blemishes on the family line and various subterfuges might be resorted to as a way of escaping the past, but no significant difference of culture or appearance limited the participation of the descendants of slaves in the culture into which they were born.

Immigration to the United States and to Israel typifies the kind of absorption in which the young are required to behave in ways that are at sharp variance with the cultural behavior of their forebears. In Israel, immigrants from Eastern Europe placed the elderly—grandparents who accompanied their adult children—on the shelf. They treated them with the lessened respect accorded those who no longer have power and with a kind of negligence that emphasized the fact that the elderly are no longer the custodians of wisdom or models for the behavior of the young.

In a postfigurative culture the young may shudder away from the infirmities of the old or they may yearn for the wisdom and power the old represent; in both cases, they themselves will become what the old now are. But for the descendants of immigrants, whether the migration was voluntary or carried out under compulsion and whether the the old people resolutely turned their backs on poverty and oppression or yearned for the life that once was theirs, the grandparents represent a past that has been left behind. Looking at their grandparents, the children see men and women whose footsteps they will never follow, but who are, by virtue of the tie through the parents, the people they would have become in another setting.

Also in slowly changing societies the small, recognizable changes in behavior by which one generation is differentiated from the last can be handled as changes in fashion, that is, as unimportant innovations by the young in matters of dress, manners, or recreation about which the old do not bother. In New Guinea, where peoples continually borrow new styles from or trade them with one another, all the women of a tribe, young and old alike, may adopt a new fashionable style of grass skirt, long in front and short behind (instead of short in front and long behind) or else the old women, who continue to wear the old outmoded skirts, may be firmly branded as old-fashioned. Minor variations within a prevailing cultural style do not essentially change the situation. In either case, girls know that they will do whatever their grandmothers have done. When they are grandmothers they, too, will take up new fashions or, alternatively, they will leave it to the young to try out successive new fashions. The idea of continuity underlies the idea of fashion. The emphasis on fashion affirms that nothing important is changed.

In New Guinea cultures, no discrimination is made between changes that have a deep relationship to the core of the culture and superficial changes that may be made many times in a lifetime without touching the core. Throughout the area there is an essential homogeneity in the traits that are available for borrowing and abandonment, and many elements that are passed from tribe to tribe have followed the same course before. Analysis of New Guinea cultures demonstrates how continuous small changes at the surface can, in fact, produce great continuity and stability at deeper levels.

In contrast, the situation in which cofiguration occurs is one in which the experience of the young generation is radically different from that of their parents, grandparents, and other older members of their immediate community. Whether the young are the first native-born generation of a group of immigrants, the first birthright members of a new religious cult, or the first generation to be reared by a group of successful revolutionaries, their progenitors can provide them with no living models suitable for their age. They themselves must develop new styles based on their own experience and provide models for their own peers. The innovations made by the children of pioneers—those who first entered the new land or the new kind of society—have the character of adaptiveness which the elders, heedful of their own inexperience in the new country or their lack of past experience in the new religious or postrevolutionary world, can interpret as a continuation of their own purposive activity. The elders did, in fact, migrate; they cut down the trees in the forest or tamed the desert and built new settlements in which children, growing up, would have new opportunities for development. And these partially oriented adults, though they may take false cues from bird songs and seasons, can glory in the better habituation of their children.

Conflict between generations in such situations is not initiated by the adults. Rather, it arises when the new methods of rearing the children are found to be insufficient or inappropriate for the formation of a style of adulthood to which the first generation, the pioneers, had hoped their children would follow.

Pioneers and immigrants who came to the United States, Canada, New Zealand, Australia, South Africa, or Israel had few precedents in their own experience on which, without conscious thought, they could base the way they reared their children. How much leeway should parents give children? How far should children be allowed to wander from home? How could parents control them, as the parents had been controlled by their fathers, by threats of disinheritance? Yet as the young grew up in these new situations, forming firm bonds among themselves, struggling with new conditions in

the outer world and with obsolescent precedents in the minds
of all their parents, their modeling on one another might still
be well below the level of articulateness. In the United
States, as one son after another, in one home after another,
disagreed with his father and left home to go West or to
some other part of the country, the circumstance that these
battles were recurrent in most households came to have the
appearance of the natural order of relations between fathers
and sons.

It is possible that in societies in which there is strong opposition between generations, expressed in an insistence on separate living arrangements or in protracted symbolic conflict
as control changes hands, the conflict originated in some
major environmental shift. Once incorporated in the culture
and taken for granted, such conflicts become part of the
postfigurative culture. Great-grandfather left home, so did
grandfather, and, in his turn, so did father. Or, inversely,
grandfather hated the school to which his father sent him; father also hated it, but in turn sent his son to the same kind of
school, fully expecting him to hate it. The occurrence of a
generation break in which the younger generation, lacking
experienced elders, must take their cues from one another is
a process that is very old in human history and recurs in any
society as the aftermath of a break in the continuity of experience. Such a cofigurative episode may then be absorbed as
the institution of age grading or the institutionalization of rebellion at a certain stage in maturation.

The situation is a very different one, however, when the
parental group has to face a change in their children and
grandchildren to a kind of behavior that already is ex-
emplified by members of some other group—a conquering
society, a dominant religious or political group, or the long-
time inhabitants of the nation into which they have come as
immigrants or of the city into which they have moved as mi-
grants. In this situation they are constrained, by external
force or by the strength of their own desires, to encourage
their children to become part of the new order—to let their

children leave them—by learning the new language, new habits, and new manners, which, from the parents' viewpoint, may have the appearance of a new set of values.

The new heritage is presented to the children by elders who are not their parents, grandparents, or members of their own transplanted or birthright settlements. Often the children have little access to the full home life characteristic of the culture to which they are asked to accommodate themselves, and their parents may have none. But as the children go to school or to work or enter the armed services, they come in contact with peers with whom they can compare themselves. These peers present them with more practical models than those of the elders—the teachers, officials, or officers whose past is inaccessible to them and whose future it is difficult for them to see as their own.

In such situations the new entrants find that their peers, who belong to the system, are the best guides. This is the case in an institution, such as a prison or a mental hospital, in which there is a marked break between the inmates or patients and the powerful administrators and their delegates. In such institutions it is usually assumed that the staff personnel —wardens and other custodians, doctors and nurses—are very different from the prisoners or patients. So newcomers model their behavior on that of older prisoners or patients.

In a caste society like that of traditional India, in which there was mobility within a caste but none between castes, members of different castes lived in close proximity within an essentially postfigurative culture. The impossibility of crossing caste lines—of acquiring the status, prerogatives, and standards of behavior of members of other castes—made it possible for the children to incorporate firmly both what they could not be and what they could be in their conception of their identity. In most societies a similar effect is attained in the upbringing of boys and girls. Members of each sex incorporate the behavior of the opposite sex as a negative ideal and reject it for themselves. In these circumstances, any crossing of sex lines—as when a man chooses an occupation that is regarded as feminine (and therefore effeminate for a man) or a woman attempts to take up a masculine occupation—produces a turmoil of generational conflict.

Moreover, in class societies in which there is a high expectation of mobility, problems of generation conflict are endemic. Young people who are moving away from the position of their parents, whether they are peasants or members of a the middle class in an aristocratic society, or members of a subordinate racial or ethnic group, must openly and consciously forsake the postfiguration provided by their parents and grandparents and seek new models. This may be accomplished in various ways. In some societies, for example, in which it is customary for a small number of villagers or peasants to go to the city and learn city ways, those who do so treat urban modes of behavior as parallel to, rather than competitive with, rural modes and do not break the ties with their own upbringing. After years of city living, the petty official retires to his original home, there to live out his days eating the same food and following the same practices as his father before him did.

But in most class societies, changes in occupation and status that entail modifications of behavior also involve changes in character structure as well. Normally, the first break with the parental style comes about in connection with education, when parents elect a different type of education and a new occupational goal for their children. The outcome, however, is determined by the situation. When the number of such young people is large, they become models for one another and, rejecting the behavior models of adults in the new environment, treat teachers and administrators as opposition forces to be outwitted, not followed. But when the number of novices or students or recruits involved in change is small, the behavior of the majority becomes their model. Or an isolated adolescent may cling to one teacher who in some measure can provide support and guidance toward an adult path.

This kind of passionate attachment of an adolescent to an adult mentor can provide great depth, but it may also alienate young individuals from their own age group. They not only fail to approximate closely the behavior of their new peers, but also give up the behavior appropriate to those of their own class or cultural group. They do not fit fully into the new setting and, returning to their place of origin, cannot re-establish ties there. In contrast, boys and girls who have entered enthusiastically into the new pursuits of school and college and who are at ease with their own age mates may be able, when they return home for short periods, to transfer that sense of ease to those at home. An isolated, adult-fixated student, returning to his home, will seem alien to his fellows; but a group of schoolboys who have developed their own style may become models for their younger brothers—and sisters also—who will find it "natural" to follow in their footsteps.

The irruption of outsiders having a different past experience into any age class inevitably will produce changes in the army, school, or monastery system; often the entire age group will come to have goals distinctly different from those of their officers, teachers, or novice-masters. The newcomers may import a style of behavior that contrasts with that of birthright members. Or, introducing new slang and new points of view, they may develop variations on the birthright style and become models for their birthright companions. In any event, cofigurative behavior in which neither past nor future is clearly envisioned and all behavior is regulated by clique or group behavior is inevitably shallow and somewhat dissociated from the postfigurative experience of childhood. Where periods away from home, designed to break the ties between adolescents and their parents and local groups, have become a standardized preparation for specific occupations, this dissociation itself becomes institutionalized. The English boarding-school boy finds it impossible to communicate very much to his parents about his school experience, even though he knows his father's experience was identical. The very identity of the alienating experience may make it a barrier between father and son.

Students of adolescence stress the conformity characteristic of this age. But the conformity they discuss occurs in one of two types of culture—in the culture in which cofigurative behavior has been institutionalized for many generations, for example, in a society with institutionalized age grading; or, in contrast, in the culture in which the majority of adolescents, finding no models in the behavior of parents whose experience is alien to theirs, must depend heavily on all the small external cues that can give them a sense of membership in a new group.

In its simplest form, a cofigurative society is one in which there are no grandparents present. Young adults, migrating from one part of a country to another, may leave their parents behind them, or they may leave them in the old country when they emigrate to a new one. Grandparents also are likely to be absent in a modern, mobile society like that of the United States, in which both old and young move frequently, or in any industrialized, highly urban society in which the affluent or the very poor segregate the elderly in special homes or areas.

The transition to a new way of life in which new skills and modes of behavior must be acquired appears to be much easier when there are no grandparents present who remember the past, shape the experience of the growing child, and reinforce, inarticulately, all the unverbalized values of the old culture. The absence of grandparents usually also means the absence of a closed, narrow ethnic community. In contrast, when grandparents are part of a group immigrating into an alien society, the close ties within a village community may serve to keep the immigrant community intact.

When young adults strike out for themselves and form new ties appropriate to a new style of life, the ties among cousins also are weakened. It is ties through the ancestral group that keep alive contacts among the younger generation. In the United States, living aunts and uncles, by keeping up relationships with their nephews and nieces, also preserve the relationships among cousins. When they die, cousin relationships attenuate.

With the removal of the grandparents physically from the world in which the child is reared, the child's experience of its future is shortened by a generation and its links to the past are weakened. The essential mark of the postfigurative culture—the reversal in an individual's relationship to his child or his relationship to his own parents—disappears. The past, once represented by living people, becomes shadowy, easier to abandon and to falsify in retrospect.

The nuclear family, that is, the family that consists only of parents and young children, is in fact a highly flexible social group in situations in which a large portion of a population or each generation in succession must learn new ways of living. It is easier to adapt to the life style of a new country or to make new adaptations when immigrants or pioneers, separated from their parents and other senior relatives, are surrounded by others of their own age group. So, also, the receiving society can draw on the special skills of individuals coming from many cultures as immigrants, when all the newcomers are learning the new language and the new technology and can reinforce one another's commitment to the new way of life.

In large organizations that must change, and change quickly, retirement is a social expression of the same need for flexibility. The removal of senior officers and elderly personnel, all those who in their persons, their memories, and their entrenched relationships to their juniors, reinforce obsolescent styles, is parallel to the removal of grandparents from the family circle.

Where grandparents are absent or lose their power to control, the young may ostentatiously ignore adult standards or assume a mien of indifference to them. Adolescents enact their limited and labeled role, with the next younger group as their audience, and full cofiguration is established in which those who provide the models are only a few years older than those who are learning.

This is happening today in New Guinea in the Manus villages in the Admiralties. In 1928 the young men who went away to work as unskilled, indentured laborers on their return were reabsorbed into the community; they were models only in the sense that, like them, younger boys wanted to go away to work and expected to return. Nowadays, however, the home-coming schoolboys and girls, with their school clothes, their transistor radios, their guitars and school books, give a coherent picture of a different life. Although there are now village elementary schools, it is the returning boarding-school adolescents who are the models for the younger boys and girls. Although the adults approve, they can do little to help the younger children establish the radically new forms of behavior.

Conditions are somewhat different in the Iatmul village of Tambunam in New Guinea, where I worked in 1938 and visited briefly in 1967 and where adolescents and young men have been going away to work for Europeans for more than fifty years. In the past they almost always went in small groups, as recruiters coming to the village "bought" eight or ten boys from complacent elders or as a group of friends ran away over their elders' protests. On plantations, in the mines, on ships, they were initiated by other work-boys, who were also part of a temporary, age-graded group, all of them far away from their villages. Here the younger boys, who had been recruited for a three-year period, entered a completely cofigurative society, the canons of which were expressed in a new language, pidgin English (now called Neo-Melanesian). Their two worlds—the work-boy world and the village home —remained distinct, and when they returned home they were reabsorbed, although with increasing difficulty, into the slowly changing life of their own villages. The dissociated nature of the work-boy experience was illustrated by the accounts they gave in response to our questions. The three years during which they conformed in dress, manners, and behavior to the work-boy style were summed up in a few brief sentences. In contrast, every detail of their terrain and way of life, including their memories of the past when their fathers still took part in head-hunting raids, was revivified as they approached home.

As the years went by, little colonies of Iatmul men from the villages were formed in the larger towns; now a few men are even taking their wives and children with them. Young men not only go away to work or to sell their carvings, but also to visit. They are beginning to find in the distant towns a small society into which they can be initiated by elders and age mates who shared the postfigurative experiences of their childhood.

Tambunam is a postfigurative culture in which men, proud of their past, set high standards both for themselves and for the school children, who, they believe, will be taught by white teachers to live as white men do. Each generation of men has adapted to change, but none has lost the sense of continuity.

Mbaan, one of the oldest men in the village, was a work-boy before World War I. Today he remains a completely traditional figure, a great expert in the old ways who also speaks fluent Neo-Melanesian and who says explicitly that when his generation has died, the past, too, will have died.

Tomi, the political leader of the village thirty years ago, had a quite different experience. Before World War I he had worked in what was then German New Guinea, not as a work-boy on a plantation, but in the home of Mrs. Parkinson, the part-Samoan wife of Richard Parkinson, the author of *Dreissig Jahre in der Südsee*. Mrs. Parkinson had helped establish a style that was transitional between the aboriginal past and the new German colonial style. His experience in her model household might have turned Tomi into an expatriated native who married and lived away from home. Instead, he returned to Tambunam, where he became politically powerful. He was adamantly opposed to missions and the proposed mission school, but he set a precedent of good relations with government. He not only spoke Neo-Melanesian fluently, but also had gained from his isolated experience an ease of communication with white people and enjoyment in managing their affairs. In 1938 he acted as our principal executive officer in the village.

In 1967 Kami Asavi, who had been the smallest boy in our household in 1938, immediately assumed Tomi's role in organizing the household we were setting up. Immediately after World War II, Kami Asavi had carried considerable responsibility as a member of the native police force charged with rounding up Japanese prisoners. Like Tomi, in whose household he had grown up as a young kinsman, he learned to enjoy an executive position among white men, but felt that his deepest ties were to his own society. He was Tomi's chosen successor. After Tomi's death, when he took over the position of village leader, he lined up the children and marched them off to school. Just as he belonged to the past, in his own eyes, they belonged to the future. School, not a model created by the young for themselves, was the way to that future. Tambunam is moving slowly through change, but the elders, even now, are not fully consciously supporting a transition stage.

So the course of change among the Iatmul contrasts with that of the Manus. The Manus, a seagoing people, already vigorously attuned to taking what they wanted in material things from their neighbors, transformed their own culture. When I studied them in 1928, I expected them to acquire a deteriorated version of the widespread shallow culture of New Guinea work-boys. Instead, in 1946, after their exposure to the Japanese and the Allied armed forces in world War II, they began to redesign their own culture and moved all three generations into their own version of Euro-American culture.

The new Manus culture was unusual in that it made possible for the whole society, transformed by a set of rules designed by its own members, to skip thousands of years. But it was not what I will describe as a prefigurative culture, because the Manus thought they were modeling their culture on one already in existence. Each small change was con-

ceived as a way of acquiring Euro-American, often specifically American, social forms. Moreover, the whole society
moved at once; unlike societies in which the elder generation is disallowed, abandoned, or eliminated, the Manus were
able to accomplish a kind of change that is unprecedented in
history. Within twelve years after the establishment of the
first school, they were contributing teachers, clerks, interpreters, and nurses to the Territory of Papua New Guinea
and were sending their first students to the new University of
Papua and New Guinea in Port Moresby. By including the
grandparents within the design for change, they retained the
strength of a postfigurative culture that was particularly well
adapted to change.

Concentration on the nuclear family, from which the
grandparents have been eliminated and in which ties to all
kin are very much weakened as is true today in most of the
industrialized or industrializing world, is typical in immigration situations in which large numbers of people move great
distances or have to adapt themselves to new, greatly contrasting styles of life. In time, this emphasis on the nuclear
family becomes incorporated in the new culture; even when
grandparents are present, their influence is minimized. It is
no longer expected that grandparents will be models for their
grandchildren or that parents will have firm control over
adult children's marriages or careers. The expectation that
children will go away from or beyond their parents—as their
own parents have done—becomes part of the culture.

When those who move to the city or to a country overseas
are all members of one culture, the locus of power lies not
with the elders, who are disregarded, but with a younger age
group, and the first generation of adapted children set a style
that may perpetuate a thinner version of the older culture. In
this kind of cofiguration, the loss of the grandparents is not
compensated for. When the adults who made the transition
reach grandparental age, they do not reconstitute, except in
isolated cult groups or aristocracies, the lost three-generation
organization. The new culture often lacks depth and variety

and, to the extent that it does, as, for example, in many ethnic enclaves in the United States or Argentina, may be less flexible and less open to adaptive change than the old postfigurative culture was. Evidence of this is found in the preservation of archaic forms of speech, in the reinstatement of kin ties on a generational basis, and in the rejection of the stranger.

In old and very complex societies, postfigurative cults or sects survive in spite of drastic social change. One example is the Hobbyhorse cult in England, in which participants wear masks reminiscent of the most primitive cultures and carry out practices handed down from one generation to the next for hundreds of years. In England and elsewhere such survivals exist side by side with the customs of the mid-twentieth century.

Over and over again in history, ways have been found to stabilize a culture within a new environment. In time, of course, there will always be a grandparental generation present, but new ways may be found of disregarding the elderly. So, for example, the technology and ceremonialism of Eskimo culture did not require the knowledge or esoteric wisdom of the elders. The Eskimo style of distant travel and visiting from one family to another made essential the development of very rapid and efficient means of orienting a hunter to a new territory. Unlike Australian aborigines, whose style of learning depended on lifelong knowledge of one territory and the endowment of that territory with tremendous supernatural significance, the Eskimo developed a style of communicating information rapidly that permitted them to move freely and easily into new territory. The old men were not needed as a repository of knowledge. Eskimo society was based on a two-generation group. When the old became a burden and a threat to the survival of the young, they themselves elected to die. Comparably, in the United States or Great Britain, at an extreme remove technologically from the Eskimo, the coal miner who has passed his prime has no active role in the limited, controlled communities inhabited exclusively by miners.

In pre-World War I Poland the landed peasant would turn over the land to his married son in return for assurances that he would care for both his parents for life. But these assurances sometimes proved to have no binding power, and the old couple might be turned out to wander as beggars on the roads.

The ease with which many second- and third-generation Americans relinquish all responsibility for the elderly is related to the loss of sanctions. The breakdown of sanctions once exercised by the old, who retained control of property until they died, may mean that the position of the old is never restored. Similarly, where the old, because of better medical care, continue to live far beyond their expected lifetimes, they may be shorn of responsibilities the next generation is more than ready to take over. Each such adaptive shift carries with it possibilities of change and a reduction of the depth characteristic of postfigurative cultures.

Under conditions of rapid change in a new country or under new conditions, men and women may relate to change in sharply contrasting ways. New ways of making a living may drastically affect the position of men who shift, for example, from full participation in a peasant community or from the narrow, controlled life of a rural sharecropper to the anonymous life of the urban unskilled laborer. But conditions may change very little for women, as they continue to cook and rear their children much as their mothers did. In these circumstances the parts of the culture that are transmitted by women in the course of forming the child's character in its early years may be conserved, while other parts of the culture, related to the drastically changed conditions of men's work, are radically altered and, in turn, lead to alterations in the character formation of children.

Cultures may be distinguished not only in terms of the relative importance of the roles played by grandparents and other kin, but also in terms of the continuity—or lack of continuity—in the form of what is passed on from grandparent to parent to grandchild. For example, where there has been a shift in living style—for one in which men went to live in their wives' communities and women remained close to their mothers to one in which daughters left their homes to live in their husbands' communities—evidence of this shift is found in discontinuities in handicraft styles. In contrast, the exceedingly conservative nature of styles of singing, evidence for which was found by Alan Lomax in his comparative studies of world song styles, can be attributed in part to the lullabies generations of mothers have sung to their children, unchanged in spite of massive changes in a people's way of life.

Conservatism in child rearing is also characteristic of those cultures in which young children care for infants and the younger ones are very close to the immediate pasts of the child nurses. Child nurses demand very little of their charges and demonstrate very little affection; they tend to carry their charges or drag them along instead of teaching them to fend for themselves. In highly complex cultures, the peasant nurses, keeping the children close to their roots and minimizing stimulation, also are characteristically conservative in their influence.

When schools are first introduced into a society that has depended upon older children as child nurses, the culture may be disrupted in several ways. The older children are cut off from the daylong learning of traditional skills and are segregated under teachers whose content and style of teaching may be entirely new. At the same time, mothers have to take over the care of infants. This happens also, of course, when peasant women are no longer available to care for the children of the well-to-do. In both cases a new element enters the situation. Mothers and fathers, both of whom have other heavy responsibilities, are much more demanding of children, less patient and willing to keep them dependent and infantilized; in addition, the models they present to children are far more skilled and complex.

The existence of a caste or class component in the upbringing of children brings about a very complex interrelationship between the two groups. In the American Southeast, where upper-class white children were reared by black nurses, white children acquired a sense of closeness to black people and the nurse learned to treat her charge differently from her own child. The kind of intimacy that existed within two such interacting groups was absent among others who, if they were white, employed no servants and, if they were black, did not work as domestic servants. Today, one of the conditions that has increased the distance and the expression of mutual hostility between blacks and whites is a new kind of segregation that has come about as fewer families employ servants, and fewer black people have close contact with the white community as nurses or caretakers or as the recipients of care formerly tendered them by white nurses and doctors or other professional persons, without new forms of contact to replace these old nurturing relationships.

In the United States the conservative and stabilizing effects of old cross-caste and cross-class relationships are disappearing rapidly. Since World War II, new residence patterns, changes in education, the refusal of many Americans to perform menial work and the opening to more of them of opportunities for entrance into other occupations, including professional occupations, all have contributed to the general breakdown of older relationships between those who conform to the standards of the core culture and those who, for reasons of color, education, social isolation, or individual choice, refuse to conform.

In each culture, only certain periods in the maturation of the growing child are selected for emphasis in child rearing; which they are may differ in the several parts of one complex society. What is emphasized in each part reflects the nature of the relationships between generations, as well as ages and classes within generations, and varies with the prevailing generation pattern. In a culture in which heavy stress is placed on early training in relation to food, the roles of the mother and grandmother are proportionately important.

Where the boy's training in the control of his body and the development of manual skills begin early and are associated with the acquisition of masculine skills, the father and grandfather become important as soon as the boy learns to walk and talk. And to the extent that male and female personalities are dichotomized, the treatment accorded boys and girls at the oedipal phase will be differentiated.

When a new cultural style is established among immigrants, when primitive or peasant peoples are brought within the direct control of national states or when new levels of literacy and technological participation are forced on a people, the stage of development on which pressure appropriate to the new style of learning falls may be different from what it was in the past. A new pressure point may come when a young man leaves home to enter the national army, when the adolescent leaves a village school to enter a regional school, or when a child of six enters a village school designed on an alien model. Or the initial impact of change may come through methods of infant care promoted among young adults by government emissaries of public health as they reach out into villages where few other changes are occurring.

Wherever cofiguration occurs—where young men are drilled to imitate fellow citizens, where boys in school are trained in new ways, or where school children are marched into village schools and educated to conform to a model developed far away in a different kind of society—the age and state of the initiates and the place and state of this group in the older postfigurative culture will be important. If the group already has incorporated the expectation of change through the upbringing of children, it may survive tremendous shifts virtually unchanged. Or, as in the case of East European Jews in the United States, the group may even accomplish a complete reversal in cultural roles. In the European style, fathers of daughters looked for promising sons-in-law; in the American style, promising young men look for the daughters of wealthy fathers. The greater the expectation of change, the less disruptive introduced cofigurations are likely to be.

As they adapted themselves to the American culture of their day, members of each non-English-speaking immigrant group had to give up their own language and specific cultural tradition. The education of the children was the principal mechanism through which this was accomplished. The parents had no control over the new learning; indeed, in most cases, they had no control over formal education in the countries from which they came. In America they had to entrust their children to the schools and accept their children's interpretation of what was correct American behavior. The children had for guidance only the precepts of their teachers and the examples of their age mates. In time, the experience of the children of immigrants became the experience of all American children, who now were the representatives of the new culture living in a new age. As such, they stood in a position of considerable authority and model setting vis-à-vis the parent generation.

The mere condition of rapid change can produce similar results. In nations such as India, Pakistan, or the new countries of Africa, children are also the authorities on the new ways and parents lose their power to judge and control. But where change occurs within a country, the combined weight of the old culture, the redintegrative power of old landmarks, and the presence of grandparents modulates the new authority claimed by the children. In countries of multiethnic immigration, however, the cofigurational effect is doubled and parents, displaced in time and space, find it doubly difficult to retain any control or even the belief that control is possible or desirable.

Where cofiguration among age mates has become institutionalized throughout the culture, one finds the phenomenon of youth culture, or "teen-age" culture; age stratification, encouraged by the school system, becomes increasingly important. In the United States, the culture-wide effects of cofiguration began to be felt by the beginning of the twentieth century. The nuclear family was established, a close relationship to the grandparents no longer was expected of grandchildren, and parents, as they lost their position of dominance, handed over to children the task of setting their own standards. By 1920, style setting was beginning to pass to the mass media, in the name of each successive adolescent group, and parental discipline was passing to the wider community. One effect of this change, by the 1960s, was the transformation of some portion of the new generation of middle-class young people into a semblance of the ethnic gangs that, in an earlier period, had battled each other and the police in our big cities. Culturally, cofiguration had become the dominant, prevailing mode. Few of the elderly pretended to have any relationship to the contemporary culture. Parents, however grudgingly, expected to accede to the urgent demands their children were taught to make, not by the school or by other, more acculturated children, but by the mass media.

Societies that make deliberate use of the possibilities of cofiguration, by inducting adolescents or adults into groups in which they were not reared or trained, are often highly flexible in making new adaptations. To the extent that formal induction, such as occurs in various types of novitiate—in initiations, in the preliminary stage of training for service in the armed forces, in training for the professions—is treated as a form of condensed childhood learning or, alternatively, as a total postfigurative experience, it is a highly successful mechanism for teaching and learning.

Individuals who have grown up in a nuclear family, in which there is only a two-generation enforcement of early expectations, know that their fathers and mothers differ from their four grandparents and that their children will grow up to be different from themselves. In contemporary societies there is the added expectation that childhood training will be at best only a partial preparation for induction into various groups other than the family. Taken together, living in a changing nuclear family and experiencing the effects of induction into new groups give the individual the sense of living in an ever-changing world. The more intense the experience of generational change in the family and of social change through involvement in new groups, the more brittle the social system becomes and the less secure the individual is likely to be. The idea of progress, which provides a rationale for the unstable situation, makes it bearable. It was the immigrant Americans' expectation that their children would be better educated and more successful than they themselves were that supported them as they struggled with the difficulties of transition.

So in a society like our own, in which there is great social mobility, there are inevitably generation breaks in education and styles of living. Nevertheless, young people, as they move up and out of their parental class, encounter certain values that are shared by most adults of the two older generations. Characteristically, these unchallenged beliefs, held by all adults, are unanalyzed, just as they are in postfigurative cultures. In an isolated society, it is relatively easy to re-establish a rigid adult consensus. But in the present-day interconnected world, it takes an iron or a bamboo curtain to assure a semblance of unanimity. Much more characteristic of contemporary societies is the disappearance of earlier forms of postfiguration. At the same time, recurrent attempts are made to re-establish unanalyzed consensus and unequivocal loyalty; or the followers of nativistic, revolutionary, or utopian cults try to form closed communities as a way of establishing for all time some desired way of life.

Also characteristic of the modern world are the acceptance of generation breaks and the expectation that each new generation will experience a technologically different world. But this expectation does not extend to a recognition that the change between generations may be of a new order. For generations two cultural groups, Jews and Armenians, have reared their children to expect to move and to learn new languages without losing their sense of cultural identity. In much the same way, children in our own and many other cultures are being reared to an expectation of *change within changelessness*. The mere admission that the values of the young generation, or of some group within it, may be different in *kind* from those of their elders is treated as a threat to whatever moral, patriotic, and religious values their parents uphold with postfigurative, unquestioning zeal or with recent, postfiguratively established, defensive loyalty.

It is assumed by the adult generation that there still is general agreement about the good, the true, and the beautiful and that human nature, complete with built-in ways of perceiving, thinking, feeling, and acting, is essentially constant. Such beliefs are, of course, wholly incompatible with a full appreciation of the findings of anthropology, which has documented the fact that innovations in technology and in the form of institutions inevitably bring about alterations in cultural character. It is astonishing to see how readily a belief in change can be integrated with a belief in changelessness, even in cultures whose members have access to voluminous historical records and who agree that history consists not merely of currently desirable constructs but of verifiable facts.

Contemporary statements about human beings' plight or, alternatively, human beings' new opportunities do not envision the emergence of new mechanisms of culture change and culture transmission that differ fundamentally from the postfigurative and cofigurative mechanisms we are familiar with. Yet I believe the new cultural form is emerging that I have called "prefiguration." As I see it, children today face a future that is so deeply unknown that it cannot be handled, as we are currently attempting to do, as a generation change with cofiguration within a stable, elder-controlled and parentally modeled culture in which many postfigurative elements are incorporated.

I believe that we can, and would do better to, apply to our present situation the pioneer model—the model of first-generation pioneer immigrants into an unexplored and uninhabited land. But for the concept of migration in space (geographical migration), I think we must substitute a new concept, migration in time.

Within two decades, 1940–60, events occurred that have irrevocably altered human beings' relationships to other human beings and to the natural world. The invention of the computer, the successful application of atomic fission and fusion in both military and civil fields, the discovery of the biochemistry of the living cell, exploration of the planet's surface, the extreme acceleration of population growth and the recognition by some of the certainty of catastrophe if it continues, the breakdown in the organization of cities, the beginning of man's destruction of his own natural environment, the linking up of all parts of the world by means of jet-propelled flight and television, the building of the first satellites and man's first ventures into space, the newly realized possibilities of unlimited atomic energy and synthetic raw materials, and, in the more advanced countries, the transformation of the age-old problems of production into problems of distribution and consumption—all these have brought about a drastic, irreversible division between the generations.

Even very recently, the elders could say: "You know, I have been young and *you* never have been old." But today's young people can reply: "You never have been young in the world I am young in, and you never can be." This is the common experience of pioneers and their children. In this sense, all of us who were born and reared before the 1940s are immigrants in today's culture. Like first-generation pioneers, we were reared to have skills and values that are only partly appropriate in this new time, but we are the elders who still command the techniques of government and power. And like immigrant pioneers from colonizing countries, we cling to the belief that the children will, after all, turn out to be much like ourselves. But balancing this hope there is the fear that the young are being transformed into strangers before our eyes, that teen-agers gathered at a street corner are to be feared like the advance guard of an invading army.

We reassure ourselves by saying: "Boys will be boys." We rationalize, telling one another that "these are very unstable times" or that "the nuclear family is very unstable" or that "children are exposed to a lot of dangerous things on television." We say the same things about our children and about new countries that, as soon as they are established, demand an airline and an embassy in every world capital: "They are young and immature. They will learn. They will grow up."

In the past, in spite of generations of cofiguration and the wide acceptance of the possibilities of rapid change, there were extreme discrepancies in what was known by people of different classes, regions, and specialized groups in any country as well as in the experiences of peoples living in different parts of the world. Change was still relatively slow and uneven. Young people living in some countries and belonging to certain class groups within a country knew more than adults living in other countries and belonging to other classes. But there were also always adults who knew more, in terms of experience, than any young people.

Today, suddenly, because all the peoples of the world are part of one electronically based, intercommunicating network, young people everywhere share a kind of experience that none of the elders ever have had or will have. Conversely, the older generation will never see repeated in the lives of young people their own unprecedented experience of sequentially emerging change. This break between generations is wholly new: it is planetary and universal.

Today's children have grown up in a world their elders never knew, but few adults knew that this would be so. Those who did know it were the forerunners of the prefigurative cultures of the future in which the prefigured is the unknown.

CHAPTER FOUR

Prefigurative Cultures and Unknown Children

The turmoil of the sixties has been variously attributed to the overwhelming rapidity of change, the collapse of the family, the decay of capitalism, the triumph of a soulless technology, and, in wholesale repudiation, to the final breakdown of the Establishment. Behind these attributions there is a more basic conflict between those for whom the present represents no more than an intensification of our existing cofigurative culture, in which peers are more than ever replacing parents as the significant models of behavior, and those who contend that we are in fact entering a totally new phase of cultural evolution.

Most commentators, in spite of their differences in viewpoint, still see the future essentially as an extension of the past. The physicist Dr. Edward Teller can still speak of the outcome of a nuclear war as a state of destruction relatively no more drastic than the ravages wrought by the Mongol conqueror Genghis Khan. Writing about the present crisis, moralists refer to the decay of religious systems in the past and historians point out that time and again civilization has survived the crumbling of empires.

Similarly, most commentators treat as no more than an extreme form of adolescent rebellion the repudiation of present and past by the dissident youth of every persuasion in every kind of society in the world. So the respected columnist Max Lerner can say, "Every adolescent must pass through two crucial periods: one when he identifies with a model—a father, an older brother, a teacher—the second when he disassociates himself from his model, rebels against him, reasserts his own selfhood." There is little substantial difference between Lerner's view and that of the social scientist David Riesman in his delineation of the autonomous man as one who emerges from the present without too sharp a break with the past.

Perhaps the most extraordinary response to youthful rebellion has been that of Chairman Mao Tse-tung of the People's Republic of China, who has attempted to turn the restive young against their parents as a way of preserving the momentum of the revolution made by the grandparent generation. Little as we understand the details of what has been going on in China, what we do know suggests a tremendous effort to transform the desire to destroy, which characterizes the attitudes of young activists all around the world, into an effective instrument for the preservation of the Chinese Communist regime. There are indications that the modern Chinese may treat such new Western technologies as electronics as parallel to processes of assimilation that have occurred many times in the long history of Chinese civilization—no more significant than a new form of metallurgy.

Theorists who emphasize the parallels between past and present in their interpretations of the Generation Gap ignore the irreversibility of the changes that have taken place since the beginning of the industrial revolution. This is especially striking in their handling of modern technological development, which they treat as comparable in its effects to the changes that occurred as one civilization in the past took over from another such techniques as agriculture, script, navigation, or the organization of labor and law.

It is, of course, possible to discuss both postfigurative and cofigurative cultures in terms of slow or rapid change without specifying the nature of the process. For example, when the children of agricultural and handicraft workers entered the first factories, this marked the beginning of an irreversible change. But the fact that accommodation to this new way of living was slow, since it was spread out over several generations, meant that the changes were not necessarily perceived to be more drastic than those experienced by the peoples who were incorporated through conquest into the Roman Empire. So also, when attention is focused on generation relationships and on the type of modeling through which a culture is transmitted, it is possible to treat as fully comparable a past situation, as when a formerly landbound people learned the techniques of fishing, and a present situation in the United States, as when the children of immigrant Haitians learn computer programming.

It is only when one specifies the nature of the process that the contrast between past and present change becomes clear. One urgent problem, I believe, is the delineation of the nature of change in the modern world, including its speed and dimensions, so that we can better understand the distinctions that must be made between change in the past and that which is now ongoing.

The primary evidence that our present situation is unique, without any parallel in the past, is that the Generation Gap is world-wide. The particular events taking place in any country—China, England, Pakistan, Japan, the United States, New Guinea, or elsewhere—are not enough to explain the unrest that stirred modern youth everywhere. Recent technological change or the handicaps imposed by its absence, revolution or the suppression of revolutionary activities, the crumbling of faith in ancient creeds or the attraction of new creeds—all these serve only as partial explanations of the particular forms taken by youth revolt in different countries. Undoubtedly, an upsurge of nationalism is more likely in a country like Japan, which is recovering from a recent defeat, or in countries that have newly broken away from their colonial past than it is, for example, in the United States. It is easier for the government of a country as isolated as China to order vast changes by edict than it is for the government of the Soviet Union, acting on a European stage, to subdue Czechoslovakian resistance. The breakdown of the family is

more apparent in the West than in the East. The speed of
change is more conspicuous and more consciously perceived
in the least and in the most industrialized countries than it is
in countries occupying an intermediate position. But all this
is, in a sense, incidental when the focus of attention is on
youthful dissidence, which is world-wide in its dimensions.

Concentration on particularities can only hinder the search
for an explanatory principle. Instead, it is necessary to strip
the occurrences in each country of their superficial, national,
and immediately temporal aspects. The desire for a liberal
form of communism in Czechoslovakia, the search for racial
equality in the United States, the desire to liberate Japan
from American military influence, the support given to excessive conservatism in Northern Ireland and Rhodesia or to the
excesses of communism in Cuba—all these are particularistic
forms. Youthful activism is common to them all.

The key question in the 1960s has been this: "What are
the new conditions that have brought about the revolt of
youth right around the world?"

The first of these conditions is the emergence of a world
community. For the first time, human beings throughout the
world, in their information about one another and responses
to one another, have become a community that is united by
shared knowledge and danger. We cannot say for certain
now that at any period in the past there was a single community made up of many small societies whose members were
aware of one another in such a way that consciousness of
what differentiated one small society from another height-
ened the self-consciousness of each constituent group. As far
as we know, no such single, interacting community has
existed within archaeological time. The largest clusters of interacting human groups were fragments of a still larger unknown whole. The greatest empires pushed their borders out-
ward into regions where there were peoples whose
languages, customs, and very appearance were unknown. In
the very partially charted world of the past, the idea that all
men were, in the same sense, human beings was either unreal

or a mystical belief. Men could think about the "fatherhood of God" and the "brotherhood of man" and biologists could argue the issue of monogenesis versus polygenesis; but what all men had in common was a matter of continuing speculation and dispute.

The events of the mid-twentieth century changed this drastically. Exploration has been complete enough to convince us that there are no humanoid types on the planet except our own species. World-wide rapid air travel and globe-encircling television satellites have turned us into one community in which events taking place in one place on the earth become immediately and simultaneously available to peoples everywhere else. No artist or political censor has time to intervene and edit as a leader is assassinated or a flag planted on the moon. The world has become a community, though it lacks as yet the forms of organization and the sanctions by which a political community can be governed.

The nineteenth-century industrial revolution replaced the cruder forms of energy. The twentieth-century scientific revolution has made it possible to multiply agricultural production manifold but also drastically and dangerously to modify the ecology of the entire planet and destroy whole species. Science has made possible, through the use of computers, a new concentration of intellectual efforts that allows men to begin the exploration of the solar system and opens a new way to simulations by means of which individuals, especially individuals working in organized groups, can transcend earlier intellectual accomplishments.

The revolution in the development of food resources is on a world-wide scale. Up to the present, in many parts of the world, the medical revolution has so increased the population that the major effect of increased, efficient food production has merely been to stave off famine. But if we are able to bring the human population into a new balance, all of humanity can be, for the first time, well nourished. The medical revolution, by reducing the pressure for population increase, has begun, in turn, to release women from the age-old ne-

cessity of devoting themselves almost completely to reproductivity and, thus, will profoundly alter the future of both
men and women and the future rearing of children.

Most importantly, these changes have taken place almost
simultaneously—within the lifetime of one generation—and
the impact of knowledge of the change is world-wide. Only
yesterday, a New Guinea native's only contact with modern
civilization may have been a trade knife that was passed
from hand to hand into his village or an airplane seen
in the sky; today, as soon as he enters the smallest New
Guinea frontier settlement, he meets the transistor radio.
Until yesterday, the village dwellers everywhere were cut off
from the urban life of their own country; today, radio and
television bring them sounds and sights of cities all over the
world.

Young people of the 1960s who are the carriers of vastly
different cultural traditions enter the present at the same
point in time. It is as if, all around the world, people were
converging on identical immigration posts, each with its identifying sign: "You are now about to enter the post-World
War II world at Gate 1 (or Gate 23, or Gate 2003, etc.)."
Whoever they are and wherever their particular point of
entry may be, all are equally immigrants into the new era—
although some come as refugees and some as castaways.

They are like the immigrants of yesterday who came as
pioneers to a new land, lacking all knowledge of what
demands the new conditions of life would make upon them.
Those who came later could take their peer groups as
models. But among the firstcomers, the young adults had as
models only their own tentative adaptations and innovations.
Their past, the culture that had shaped their understanding
—their thoughts, their feelings, and their conceptions of the
world—was no sure guide to the present. And the elders
among them, bound to the past, could provide no models for
the future.

Today, everyone born and bred before World War II is an
immigrant in time—as his colonizing forebears were in space

—struggling to grapple with the unfamiliar conditions of life in a new era. Like all immigrants and pioneers, these immigrants in time are the bearers of older cultures. The difference today is that they are represented in all the cultures of the world. And all of them, whether they are sophisticated French intellectuals or members of a remote New Guinea tribe, landbound peasants in Haiti or nuclear physicists, have certain characteristics in common.

Whoever we are, we immigrants of the older generation, we grew up under skies across which no satellite had flashed. Our perception of the past was an edited version of what had happened. Whether we were wholly dependent on oral memory, art, and drama or also had access to print and still photography and film, what we could know had been altered by the very act of preservation. Our perception of the immediate present was limited to what we could take in through our own eyes and ears and to the edited versions of each other's sensory experiences and memories. Our conception of the future was essentially one in which change was incorporated into a deeper changelessness. The New Guinea native, entering the complex modern world, followed cultural models provided by Europeans and expected in some way to share their future. The industrialist or military planner, envisaging what a computer, not yet constructed, might make possible, treated it as another addition to the repertoire of inventions that have enhanced human beings' skills. It expanded what human beings could do, but did not change the future.

Mid-twentieth-century science fiction, written by young writers with little experience of human life, rang untrue to the sophisticated and experienced ear and was less interesting to most well-educated people than such myths as those of Icarus and Daedalus, which include people and gods as well as the mechanisms of flight. Most scientists shared the lack of prescience of other members of their generation and failed to share the dreams of modern science-fiction writers.

When the first atomic bomb was exploded at the end of World War II, only a few individuals realized that all humanity was entering a new age. And to this day the majority of those who are older than thirty-five have failed to grasp emotionally, however well they may grasp it intellectually, the difference between any war in which, no matter how terrible the casualties, mankind will survive and one in which there will be no human survivors. They continue to think that a war, fought with more lethal weapons, would just be a worse war; they still do not grasp the implications of scientific weapons of extinction. Even scientists, when they form committees, are apt to have as their goal not the total abolition of war, but the prevention of the particular kinds of warfare for which they themselves feel an uncomfortable special responsibility—such as the use of defoliants in Vietnam.

In this sense, then, of having moved into a present for which none of us was prepared by our understanding of the past, our interpretations of ongoing experience, or our expectations about the future, all of us who grew up before World War II are pioneers, immigrants in time who have left behind our familiar worlds to live in a new age under conditions that are different from any we have known. Our thinking still binds us to the past—to the world as it existed in our childhood and youth. Born and bred before the electronic revolution, most of us do not realize what it means.

We still hold the seats of power and command the resources and the skills necessary to keep order and organize the kinds of societies we know about. We control the educational systems, the apprenticeship systems, the career ladders up which the young must climb, step by step. The elders in the advanced countries control the resources needed by the young and less-advanced countries for their development. Nevertheless, we have passed the point of no return. We are committed to life in an unfamiliar setting; but we are still making do with what we know. We are building makeshift dwellings in old patterns with new and better understood materials.

The young generation, however, the articulate young

rebels all around the world who are lashing out against the
controls to which they are subjected, are like the first generation born into a new country. They are at home in this time.
Satellites are familiar in their skies. They have never known
a time when war did not threaten annihilation. Those who
use computers do not anthropomorphize them; they know
that they are programmed by human beings. When they are
given the facts, they can understand immediately that continued pollution of the air and water and soil will soon make
the planet uninhabitable and that it will be impossible to
feed an indefinitely expanding world population. They can
see that control of conception is feasible and necessary. As
members of one species in an underdeveloped world community, they recognize that invidious distinctions based on race
and caste are anachronisms. They insist on the vital necessity
of some new form of social order.

They live in a world in which events are presented to them
in all their complex immediacy; they are no longer bound by
the simplified linear sequences dictated by the printed word.
In their eyes the killing of an enemy is not qualitatively
different from the murder of a neighbor. They cannot reconcile our efforts to save our own children by every known
means with our readiness to destroy the children of others
with napalm. Old distinctions between peacetime and wartime, friend and foe, "my" group and "theirs"—the outsiders', the aliens'—have lost their meaning. They know that
the people of one nation alone cannot save their own children; each holds the responsibility for the others' children.

Although I have said "they know" these things, perhaps I
should say that this is *how they feel*. Like the first generation
born in a new country, they listen only half-comprehendingly
to their parents' talk about the past. For as the children of pioneers had no access to the memories which could still move
their parents to tears, the young today cannot share their
parents' responses to events that deeply moved them in the
past. But this is not all that separates the young from their
elders. Watching, they can see that their elders are groping,

that they are managing clumsily and often unsuccessfully the
tasks imposed on them by the new conditions. The children
of the early immigrants had no firsthand knowledge of the
way their parents had lived far across the seas, of how
differently wood responded to tools, or land to hoe. So today,
young people see that their elders are using means that are
inappropriate, that their performance is poor, and the outcome very uncertain. The young do not know what must be
done, but they feel that there must be a better way.

Just how they do feel has been expressed in an essay by
Shannon Dickson, a fifteen-year-old Texan boy:

> There is a mass confusion in the minds of my generation
> in trying to find a solution for ourselves and the world
> around us.
>
> We see the world as a huge rumble as it swiftly goes by
> with wars, poverty, prejudice, and the lack of under-
> standing among people and nations.
>
> Then we stop and think: there must be a better way and
> we have to find it.
>
> We see the huge rat race of arguing people trying to
> beat their fellow man out. All of this builds up, causing un-
> rest between nations and in the home. My generation is
> being used almost like a machine. We are to learn to set
> standards, strive for better education so we can follow in
> our elders' footsteps. But why? If we are to be a generation
> of repetition, the situation will be worse. But how shall we
> change? We need a great deal of love for everyone, we
> need a universal understanding among people, we need to
> think of ourselves and to express our feelings, but that is
> not all. I have yet to discover what else we need, nor have
> I practiced these things as fully as I should. Because when
> I try I'm sneered at by my elders and those who do not
> hear, or look at it with a closed mind. Computers take the
> place of minds; electronics are taking over, only confusing
> things more.

I admit we should follow some basic rules but first you should look at who is making the rules.

Sometimes I walk down a deserted beach listening to the waves and birds and I hear them forever calling and forever crying and sometimes we feel that way but everyone goes on with his own little routines, afraid to stop and listen for fear of cracking their nutshell.

The answer is out there somewhere. We need to search for it.

They feel that there must be a better way and that they must find it.

Today, nowhere in the world are there elders who know what the children know, no matter how remote and simple the societies are in which the children live. In the past there were always some elders who knew more than any children in terms of their experience of having grown up within a cultural system. Today there are none. It is not only that parents are no longer guides, but that there are no guides, whether one seeks them in one's own country or abroad. There are no elders who know what those who have been reared within the last twenty years know about the world into which they were born.

We elders are separated from them by the fact that we, too, are a strangely isolated generation. No generation has ever known, experienced, and incorporated such rapid changes, watched the sources of power, the means of communication, the definition of humanity, the limits of the explorable universe, the certainties of a known and limited world, the fundamental imperatives of life and death—all change before our eyes. We know more about change than any generation has ever known, but we also stand over against and vastly alienated from the young who, by the very nature of their position, have had to reject their elders' past.

Just as the early Americans had to teach themselves not to daydream of the past but to concentrate on the present and so in turn taught their children not to daydream but to act, so today's elders have to treat their own past as incommunicable and teach their children, even in the midst of lamenting that it is so, not to ask, because they can never understand. We have to realize that no other generation will ever experience what we have experienced. In this sense, we must recognize that we have no descendants, as our children have no forebears.

At this breaking point between two radically different and closely related groups, both are inevitably very lonely, as we face each other knowing that they will never experience what we have experienced and that we can never experience what they have experienced.

The situation that has brought about this radical change will not occur again in any such drastic form in the foreseeable future. Once we have discovered that this planet is inhabited by only one human species this cannot be disavowed. The sense of responsibility for the existence of the entire living world, once laid upon our shoulders, will not be lifted. The young will, we can hope, be prepared to educate their own children for change. But just because this Gap is unique, because nothing like it has ever occurred before, the elders are set apart from any previous generation and from the young.

This sense of distance, this feeling of lacking a living connection with members of the other generation, sometimes takes bizarre forms. In the summer of 1968 a group of American clergy who were meeting in Uppsala, Sweden, talked with some of the young American conscientious objectors to the Vietnam war who had taken refuge in Sweden, and in a written report they said: "We are persuaded that these are our children." They could not take their cultural paternity for granted, but had to persuade themselves that it was so— after long discussion. So incredible it seemed—to believe that any of their children could leave the United States, where, in the past, the persecuted of Europe had taken refuge. They spoke almost as if a process of blood typing had had to be introduced to prove their spiritual paternity.

In most discussions of the Generation Gap, the alienation of the young is emphasized, while the alienation of their elders may be wholly overlooked. What the commentators forget is that true communication is a dialogue and that both parties to the dialogue lack a common vocabulary.

We are familiar with the problems of communication between speakers of two languages who have been reared in radically different cultures—one, for example, in China and the other in the United States. Not only language but also the incommensurability of their experience prevent them from understanding each other. Yet a willingness to learn the other's language and to explore the premises of both cultures can open the way to conversation. It can be done, but it is not often done.

The problem becomes more difficult, because it is more subtle, when speakers from two different cultures share what is regarded as a common tongue, such as English for Americans and Englishmen, Spanish for Spaniards and Latin Americans. Then true communication becomes possible only when both realize that they speak not one but two languages in which some of the "same" words have divergent, sometimes radically different meanings. Then, if they are willing to listen and to ask, they can begin to talk, and talk with delight.

This is also the problem of the two generations. Once the fact of a deep, new, unprecedented world-wide Generation Gap is firmly established in the minds of both the young and the old, communication can be established again. But as long as adults think that they, like the parents and teachers of old, need only to become introspective, to invoke their own youth, to understand the youth before them, communication is impossible.

But this is what most elders are still doing. The fact that they delegate authority—that parents send their children away to school to learn new ideas, that older scientists send

their pupils to other laboratories to work on newer problems
—changes nothing. It only means that parents and teachers
are continuing to use the mechanisms of cofiguration characteristic of a world in which parents, having given up the
right to teach their own children, expect their children to
learn from other adults and their more knowledgeable age
mates. Even in science, where we have tried to build in the
expectation of discovery and innovations, students learn from
old models, and young scientists work to fill in blank spaces
in accepted paradigms. In today's accelerating rate of
scientific discovery, the old are outmoded rapidly and replaced by near peers, but still within a framework of authority.

In the deepest sense, now as in the past, the elders are still
in control. And partly because they are in control, they do
not realize that the conditions for beginning a new dialogue
with the young do not yet exist.

Ironically, it is often those who were, as teachers, very close
to former generations of students, who now feel that the Generation Gap cannot be bridged and that their devotion to
teaching has been betrayed by the young who cannot learn
in the old ways.

From one point of view the situation in which we now find
ourselves can be described as a crisis in faith, in which
human beings, having lost their faith not only in religion but
also in political ideology and in science, feel they have been
deprived of every kind of security. I believe this crisis in
faith can be attributed, at least in part, to the fact that there
are now no elders who know more than the young themselves about what the young are experiencing. C. H. Waddington, the Scottish geneticist, has hypothesized that one
component of human evolution and the capacity for choice is
the ability of the human child to accept on authority from
elders the criteria for right and wrong. The acceptance of the
distinction between right and wrong by children is a conse-
quence of their dependence on parental figures who are
trusted, feared, and loved, who hold each child's very life in

their hands. But today the elders can no longer present with certainty moral imperatives to the young.

True, in many parts of the world the parental generation still lives by a postfigurative set of values. From parents in such cultures children may learn that there have been unquestioned absolutes, and this learning may carry over into later experience as an expectation that absolute values can and should be re-established. Nativistic cults, dogmatic religious and political movements flourish most vigorously at the point of recent breakdown of postfigurative cultures and least in those cultures in which orderly change is expected to occur within a set of stable values at higher levels of abstraction.

The older industrialized countries of the West have incorporated in their cultural assumptions the idea of change without revolution through the development of new social techniques to deal with the conditions brought about by economic change and technological advances. In these same countries, obsolescence tends to be treated as survival, loved or deprecated, as the case may be. In nineteenth-century England, the messenger who carried a dispatch case to France was retained long after the dispatches were sent by post; in France, too, the pageantry of the throne exists side by side with the parliamentary government that has long superseded the throne as the source of power. In Sweden the most modern laws about sex behavior coexist with the most uncompromising orthodox religious support of an absolute morality.

Similarly, in the United States there is both a deep commitment to developmental change, which is interpreted as progress, and a continuing resort to absolutism, which takes many forms. There are the religious sects and minor political groups, the principal appeal of which is their dogmatism with regard to right and wrong. There are the utopian communes that have been a constant feature of our social, political, and intellectual development. And there is the tacit acceptance of a color caste system that exists in violation of our declared belief in the fundamental equality of all men.

Elsewhere in the world where change has been rapid, abrupt, and often violent, where the idea of orderly processes of change has not taken hold, there is a continuing possibility of sudden eruptions that may take the form of revolutions and counterrevolutions—as in most Latin-American countries —or may bring about, in sudden reversal—even though in a new form—the re-establishment of an archaic orthodoxy in which nonbelievers may be persecuted, tortured, and burned alive. The young people today who turn themselves into living torches mirror in very complex ways both the attitudes of orthodox absolutism and reactions to it. They follow the example of those Buddhists who responded to the dogmatisms of communism and reactive anticommunism with an extreme violation of their own permissive and unabsolute religious values. But their acts also represent, implicitly, the treatment accorded heretics and nonbelievers by any absolutist system that allows no appeal from its dogmas.

There are still parents who answer a child's questions— "Why must I go to bed? or eat my vegetables? or stop sucking my thumb? or learn to read?"—with simple assertions, "Because it is *right* to do so . . . because *God* says so . . . because *I* say so." These parents are preparing the way for the re-establishment of postfigurative elements in the culture. But these elements will have to be far more rigid and intractable than in the past because they must be defended in a world in which conflicting points of view, rather than orthodoxies, are prevalent and accessible.

Most parents, however, are too uncertain to assert old dogmatisms. They do not know how to teach these children who are so different from what they themselves once were, and most children are unable to learn from parents and elders they will never resemble. In the past, in the United States, the American-born children of immigrant parents pleaded with them not to speak their foreign language in public and not to wear their outlandish, foreign clothes. The children knew the burning shame of being, at the same time, unable to repudiate their parents and unable to accept simply and naturally their parents' way of speaking and doing things. But in time the children learned to find new teachers as guides, to model their behavior on that of more adapted age mates, and to slip in, unnoticed, among a group whose parents were more bearable.

Today, the dissident young discover very rapidly that this solution is no longer possible. The breach between themselves and their parents also exists between themselves and their teachers. There are no bearable answers in the old books or in the brightly colored, superficially livened-up, new textbooks they are asked to study.

Some of the dissident young look abroad for models. They are attracted by the writing of the French novelist Albert Camus, who, in his conflict between his Algerian birth and his intellectual allegiance to France, expressed some of the conflict they feel; but he is dead. They try to adapt to their own purposes the words of an aging German-born Marxist, Herbert Marcuse, or the writings of the existentialists. They develop cultist attitudes of desperate admiration for the heroes of other young revolutionary groups. White students ally themselves with the black separatists. Black students attempt to restructure the past in their struggle to restructure the present.

These young dissidents realize the critical need for immediate world action on problems that affect the whole world. What they want is, in some way, to begin all over again. The idea of orderly, developmental change is lost for this generation of young, who cannot take over the past from their elders and can only repudiate what their elders are doing now. The past for them is a colossal, unintelligible failure and the future may hold nothing but the destruction of the planet. Caught between the two, they are ready to make way for something new by a kind of social bulldozing—like the bulldozing in which every tree and feature of the landscape is destroyed to make way for a new community. Awareness of the reality of the crisis (which is, in fact, perceived most accurately not by the young but by their discerning and prophetic elders) and the sense the young have that their elders do not understand the modern world because they do not understand rebellion creates a situation in which planned reformation of the present system is almost inconceivable.

Nevertheless, those who have no power also have no routes to power except through those against whom they are rebelling. In the end, it was men who gave the vote to women; and in England it will be the House of Lords that votes to abolish the House of Lords; and it will be those over eighteen who have to agree if those under eighteen are to vote, as also, in the final analysis, nations will act to limit national sovereignty. Effective, rapid evolutionary change, in which no one is guillotined and no one is forced into exile, depends on the co-operation of a large number of those in power with the dispossessed who are seeking power. The innovating idea may come from others, but the initiative for successful action must come from those whose privileges, now regarded as obsolete, are about to be abolished.

There are those among the dissident young who recognize this. Significantly, they want their parents or those who represent their parents—deans and college presidents and editorial writers—to be on their side, to agree with them, or at least to give them a blessing. Behind their demands is their hope that, even as they demonstrate against the college administration, the college president will come and talk with them—and bring his children. But there are also some who entertain no such hope.

I have spoken mainly about the most articulate young people, those who want to drop out of the whole system and those who want to take the system apart and start over. But the feeling that nothing out of the past is meaningful and workable is very much more pervasive. Among the less articulate it is expressed in such things as the refusal to learn at school, to co-operate at work, or to follow normal political paths. Perhaps most noncompliance is of this passive kind. But the periodic massing of students behind their more active peers suggests that even passive noncompliance can be transformed into activity.

Resistance among the young is also expressed by an essentially uninvolved and exploitative compliance with rules that are regarded as meaningless. Perhaps those who take this stand are the most frightening. Going through the forms by which men were educated for generations but which no longer serve to educate those who accept them can only teach students to regard all social systems in terms of exploitation.

But whatever stand they take, few of the young, neither the most idealistic nor the most cynical, are untouched by the sense that there are no adults anywhere in the world from whom they can learn what the next steps should be.

These, in brief, are the conditions of our time. These are the two generations—pioneers in a new era and their elders who have as yet to find a way of communicating about the world in which both live, though their perceptions of it are so different. No one knows what the next steps should be. Recognizing that this is so is, I submit, the beginning of an answer.

For I believe we are on the verge of developing a new kind of culture, one that is as much a departure in style from cofigurative cultures, as the institutionalization of cofiguration in orderly—and disorderly—change was a departure from the postfigurative style. I call this new style *prefigurative,* because in this new culture it will be the child—and not the parent or grandparent—that represents what is to come. Instead of the erect, white-haired elder who, in postfigurative cultures, stood for the past and the future in all their grandeur and continuity, the unborn child, already conceived but still in the womb, must become the symbol of what life will be like. This is a child whose sex and appearance and capabilities are unknown. This is a child who may be a genius or may suffer from some deep impairment, but who will need imaginative, innovative, and dedicated adult care far beyond any we give today.

About the unborn child little can be known with certainty. We can tell with delicate instruments that supplement the ear that the child is alive, that its heart is beating. Other instruments, still more delicate, can give some clues as to the child's well-being. We can predict the approximate time when it will be born. We know that unless the mother is protected, nourished, and cared for, the child's chance for life will sink with her own; should she sicken and die, the child's life will also flicker out. But all else is unknown.

No one can know in advance what the child will become—how swiftly his limbs will move, what will delight his eye, whether his tempo will be fast or slow, whether he will waken ready to cope with the world or only reach his best hours when the day people are tiring. No one can know how his mind will work—whether he will learn best from sight or sound or touch or smell or movement. But knowing what we do not know and cannot predict, we can construct an environment in which a child, still unknown, can be safe and can grow and discover itself and the world.

In a safe and flexible environment there must be skilled care, anesthetics, oxygen, and blood on hand to protect the mother and the child in a difficult birth. There must be supportive care for the mother who becomes depressed or frightened. There must be artificial food for the infant who cannot be breast-fed. For the child who is sensitive to sound, there must be ways of muting noise.

As children begin to reach out to people, they must be carried—held or propped or cradled—into company. As their eyes respond to color, there must be many colors, differing in hue, saturation, and brightness, for them to choose among. There must be many kinds of objects for them to classify, many rhythms and melodies to start them dancing. And as they begin to form an image of the world, they must have examples of the worlds that other people have made and be given crayons and paints and clay so they can give form to the world of their own imaginations.

Even so simple an enumeration of ways of meeting a

child's needs makes us conscious of how much children have been bound to the ways of their forebears through love and dependence and trust. It also makes us conscious of how little flexibility there is in the child's dependence on adults as compared to the great flexibility that can be developed in the adult's succoring care. Without adult care, the child will never learn to speak. Without the experience of trust, the child will never become a trusting member of society, who is able to love and care for others. The child is wholly dependent, and it is on this dependency that human culture has been built as, generation after generation for hundreds of thousands of years, adults have imposed on children, through their care for them, their vision of what life should be. Dependency has made conscience possible, and, as both the English biologist Julian Huxley and Waddington have argued so eloquently, ethics are not external to nature but are crucial to human evolution.

The continuity of culture and the incorporation of every innovation depended on the success of the postfigurative system by which the young were taught to replicate the lives of their ancestors. Then, as men learned to live in many different environments and as they traveled and traded with one another, contrasts among different postfigurative cultures began to provide the necessary conditions for change and for the development of cofigurative cultures in which people who had been reared to one form of commitment learned to adapt themselves to other forms but with the same absolute commitment.

Later, as the idea of change became embodied as a postfigurative element in many cultures, the young could learn from their elders that they should go beyond them—achieve more and do different things. But this "beyond" was always within the informed imagination of their elders; the son might be expected to cross the seas his father never crossed, study nuclear physics when his father had only an elementary school education, fly in the plane which his father had watched from the ground. The peasant's son became a scholar; the poor man's son crossed the ocean his father had never seen; the schoolteacher's son or daughter became a scientist.

Love and trust, based on dependency and answering care, made it possible for the individuals who had been reared in one culture to move into another, transforming without destroying their earlier learning. It is seldom the first generation of voluntary immigrants and pioneers who cannot meet the demands of a new environment. Their previous learning carries them through. But unless they embody what is new postfiguratively, they cannot pass on to their children what they themselves had acquired through their own early training—the ability to learn from others the things their parents could not teach them.

Now, in a world in which there are no more knowledgeable "others" to whom parents can commit the children they themselves cannot teach, parents feel uncertain and helpless. Still believing that there should be answers, parents ask, "How can we tell our children what is right?" So some parents try to solve the problem by advising their children very vaguely, "You will have to figure that out for yourselves." And some parents ask, "What are the others doing?" But this resource of a cofigurative culture is becoming meaningless to parents who feel that the "others"—their children's age mates—are moving in ways that are unsafe for their own children to emulate and who find that they do not understand what their children work out for themselves.

It is the adults who still believe that there is a safe and socially approved road to a kind of life they themselves have not experienced who react with the greatest anger and bitterness to the discovery that what they had hoped for no longer exists for their children. These are the parents, the trustees, the legislators, the columnists, and commentators who denounce most vocally what is happening in schools and colleges and universities in which they had placed their hopes for their children.

Today, as we are coming to understand better the circular

processes through which culture is developed and transmitted, we recognize that a human being's most human characteristic is not the ability to learn, which human beings share with many other species, but the ability to teach and store what others have developed and taught them. Learning, which is based on human dependency, is relatively simple. But human capacities for creating elaborate, teachable systems, for understanding and utilizing the resources of the natural world, and for governing society and creating imaginary worlds—all these are very complex. In the past, human beings relied on the least elaborate part of the circular system, the dependent learning by children, for continuity of transmission and for the embodiment of the new. Now, with our greater understanding of the process, we must cultivate the most flexible and complex part of the system—the behavior of adults. We must, in fact, teach ourselves how to alter adult behavior so that we can give up postfigurative upbringing, with its tolerated cofigurative components, and discover prefigurative ways of teaching and learning that will keep the future open. We must create new models for adults who can teach their children not *what* to learn but *how* to learn, not *what* they should be committed to but the *value* of commitment.

Postfigurative cultures, which focused on the elders—those who had learned the most and were able to do the most with what they had learned—were essentially closed systems that continually replicated the past. We must now move toward the creation of open systems that focus on the future—and so on children, those whose capacities are least known and whose choices must be left open.

In doing this, we explicitly recognize that the paths by which we came into the present can never be traversed again. The past is the road by which we have arrived where we are. Older forms of culture have provided us with the knowledge, the techniques, and the tools necessary for our contemporary civilization. Coming by different roads out of the past, all the peoples of the earth are now arriving in the

new world community. No road into the present need be
repudiated and no former way of life forgotten. But all these
different pasts, our own and all others, must be treated as
precursors.

It is significant how extremely difficult it has been even for
the prophetic writers of science fiction to imagine and accept
an unknown future. At the close of *Childhood's End,* the
English author and scientist Arthur Clarke wrote: "The stars
are not for men."

Space operas picture the return of the last broken spaceship
from imagined galactic societies to the "hall of the beginning"
on Terra of Sol. In his *Midwich Cuckoos,* the British author
John Wyndham killed off the strange, golden-eyed, perceptive children bred by earth women to visitors from outer
space. Stanley Kubrick's 1968 film *2001: A Space Odyssey*
ends in failure. This deep unwillingness to have children go
too far into the future suggests that the adult imagination,
acting alone, remains fettered to the past.

So the freeing of the human imagination from the past
depends, I believe, on the development of a new kind of
communication with those who are most deeply involved
with the future—the young who were born in the new world.
That is, it depends on the direct participation of those who,
up to now, have not had access to power and whose nature
those in power cannot fully imagine. In the past, in
cofigurational cultures, the elders were gradually cut off
from limiting the future of their children. Now, as I see it,
the development of prefigurational cultures will depend on
the existence of a continuing dialogue in which the young,
free to act on their own initiative, can lead their elders in the
direction of the unknown. Then the older generation will
have access to the new experiential knowledge, without
which no meaningful plans can be made. It is only with the
direct participation of the young, who have that knowledge,
that we can build a viable future.

Instead of directing their rebellion toward the retrieval of
a grandparental utopian dream, as the Maoists did with the

young activists in China, we must learn together with the young how to take the next steps. Out of their new knowledge—new to the world and new to us—must come the questions to those who are already equipped by education and experience to search for answers.

Archibald MacLeish wrote in 1928 in *The Hamlet of A. MacLeish,*

> We have learned the answers, all the answers:
> It is the question that we do not know.

His book was sent to me that year while I was in the Admiralties, studying the Manus. At that time it seemed almost certain that the Manus, a people still proudly adapted to their stone-age culture, whose only experience of another kind of civilization was with the dehumanizing and degrading contact-culture, would eventually become poorly educated proletarians in a world they could neither understand nor influence.

Today, forty years later, the Manus people have skipped thousands of years and been able to take their destiny in their own hands, as they could not in the days when, locked within the stone age, they bullied and ravaged the villages of their less aggressive neighbors. Today they are preparing their children for college, for law schools and medical schools, and transferring the leadership they once exercised, fitfully and with poor organization, in a tiny archipelago, as a tribe, into the wider world of a developing nation. And today, when the quotation came back to me, I would, were it mine, phrase it differently because now we can say that we *do* know at least who must ask the questions if we, who have a long heritage of answers at our disposal, are to be able to answer them. The children, the young, must ask the questions that we would never think to ask, but enough trust must be re-established so that the elders will be permitted to work with the young on the answers. As in a new country with makeshift shelters adapted hastily from out-of-date models, the children must be able to proclaim that they are

cold and where the drafts are coming from; but father is still
the man who has the skill and the strength to cut down the
tree to build a different kind of house.

During the last few years, I have been exposed to something that I at first branded as a temptation. Young people
sometimes turn to me, when we have been co-operating
vividly in a goal we share, and say, "You belong to us." This
I felt to be a temptation which must be resisted at all costs,
especially in a country where youth, in every form, is a
tempting refuge for the middle-aged and aging. So I used to
reply, "No, I do not belong to your generation. You think I
do because you are currently in favor of things that I have
been working on for forty years. But that does not make me
a member of your generation. And how do I know that you
will not, in fact, be opposing these very goals ten years from
now?" But I think that this reply was another example of our
insistence that the future will be like the past, that most people go through cycles of revolt and reaction, that experience
in the past can be applied to the future. Because I made that
assumption I failed to see that perhaps they may have been
saying something different. I was reared, as they wish they
had been, by a grandmother and parents who did not think
they could set their children's feet on any given path. I was
reared almost seven decades ahead of my time, as today's
twenty-year-olds proclaim they will rear their children, leaving them free to grow, straight and tall, into a future that
must be left open and free. It is in a sense as a tribute to
such a childhood that I am able to insist that we can change
into a prefigurative culture, consciously, delightedly, and in-
dustriously, rearing unknown children for an unknown
world.

But to do this we, the peoples of the world, must relocate
the future. For the Euro-American culture the future has lain
ahead of us, sometimes only a few hours ahead, not here yet,
beyond our reach. For many Oceanic peoples, the future lies
behind, not before. For the Balinese the future is like an exposed but undeveloped film, slowly unrolling, while people

stand and wait for what will be revealed. It is seen catching up with them, a figure of speech that we, too, use when we speak of hearing time's relentless footsteps behind us.

If we are to build a prefigurative culture in which the past is instrumental rather than coercive, we must change the location of the future. Here again we can take a cue from the young who seem to want instant utopias. They say: *The future is now.*" This seems unreasonable and impetuous, and in some of the demands they make it is unrealizable in concrete detail; but here again, I think they give us the way to reshape our thinking. We must place the future, like the unborn child in the womb of a woman, within a community of men, women, and children, among us, already here, already to be nourished and succored and protected, already in need of things for which, if they are not prepared before it is born, will come too late. So, as the young say, THE FUTURE IS NOW.

PART II

From the Perspective
of the 1970s

CHAPTER FIVE

The Domestication of the
Generation Gap

In the 1960s young people, the first young people of the new generation, believed they could make the world new overnight. Children of electricity and electronics, they were accustomed to pushing buttons so that there would be light. And, as their instant aspirations erupted at a hundred universities and colleges all over the world, we, their elders, were forced to respond with violent opposition and coercion. In some places youngsters with long hair were forbidden to attend school or were threatened by motorists on the streets of American towns. Traveling youngsters with beards were deported from some countries they visited. Some youngsters, faced with opportunities to sit in the councils of their elders, screeched obscene words in total rejection. Dropping out became routine, and truant officers threw up their hands.

Some older people greeted the new order with varying degrees of enthusiasm and identification; some proclaimed the coming of the counterculture, the greening of America, and dressed and spoke like those much younger than themselves. Hope and fear dominated them, as fear of the past and hope for the immediate results of their protests dominated the articulate young. Now, in more sober retrospect, we can take stock of what has happened since the 1960s, assess what is left of those hopes and fears, and take another long look at the present, realizing even more acutely, just how unpredictable the future was.

For in 1969 I, too, was writing out of the tremendous experience that made the Generation Gap, out of the realization that something incredibly vast and irreversible had happened to the whole world, as the earth became Planet Earth, our only home, and all the people of the planet became one intercommunicating whole. In those days—for they seem almost as far off now as the "once upon a time" of a fairy tale —audiences used to ask me, "Won't there be another Generation Gap like this one as great new technological changes take place?" I constructed an answer which carried some of the needed weight: "If we should be able to colonize the moon with young adults from Earth, and children were born there who had never seen Earth, and some disaster destroyed Earth so the children could never see it, the gap between those born on Earth and those born on the moon might be as great." When an audience was still uncomprehending, turning over in their minds the stubborn belief that what had been would always be, I sometimes could capture their imaginations for a moment by saying: "When we of the other side of the Gap were children and played hide-and-go-seek, we counted by fives—"five, ten, fifteen, twenty, twenty-five, thirty"—five hundred by fives, and then "Here I come." But today, children count "ten, nine, eight, seven, six—" At about this point an American audience explodes into laughter, experiencing the significance of having grown up in a different world.

It continued to be very difficult for people to comprehend a generation gap that ringed the earth, a gap that separated all those born and reared before the mid-1940s and all those reared since. When this book was first published, angry critics wrote letters pointing out how much more they knew than the young, thinking that I was speaking of knowledge or wisdom, rather than of difference in experience. First-generation Americans, who, once they have become truly committed Americans in feeling, are the least critical of the country they have adopted, explained loftily, "I didn't get on with my father, he didn't get on with his father, and I don't expect to get on with my son, but there is nothing new about that." My French friends, forgetting their exuberance in the year of the

May 1968 extravagances, said a greater gap had been created in France by World War I.

At the beginning of the 1970s the student movements seemed to be dying out. The adults who had shared the students' hope that the world might be made new overnight were disgruntled and disappointed; others were secretly gleeful because they believed the enemy had been routed. In the summer of 1970, after the last great outbursts in the United States of youthful outrage over Cambodia and the Kent State and Jackson State massacres, the newspapers began to announce the end of student activism as a death of the spirit. They did not realize that the Generation Gap no longer coincided with the years of undergraduate study.

What was happening was very like what happened in 1945 when the atomic bomb first became part of our consciousness. We were beginning to domesticate the Generation Gap, to ignore its importance, to rob it of meaning, just as twenty-five years before, we had managed to ignore and domesticate the bomb. When the news of the bomb first broke on an unprepared and astounded world, the American editor and critic Norman Cousins wrote in *The Saturday Review* "Is Modern Man Obsolete?" sensing fully that a new era had begun, an era in which human beings might indeed be as obsolete as dinosaurs. We, who in the past had lagged centuries behind events in our power to comprehend and name them, named the "atomic age" almost overnight.

I had a book half finished that summer of 1945 when the news of Hiroshima struck, and an epoch of civilization as we had known it ended for all those who had eyes to see and ears to hear. I tore up my half-finished manuscript, knowing that not a single sentence would ring true in the new atomic age. There were flurries of activity spearheaded by those who felt most responsible—the atomic physicists themselves. For a brief few weeks, which for some hopeful prophets extended into months and years, the responsible members of society had an opportunity which they had never had before of constructing a warless world. Those of us who were human scientists struggled with ways to make what had happened intelligible to those who persisted in thinking that we were only talking about another and worse war, possibly a war that would end more quickly. "You would never know what hit you" was a typical optimistic American response to the first news of Hiroshima. The difference between the possible destruction of a large part of the world along with a large part of its people and of *all* the world's people—possibly of *all living things*—simply failed to register. People talked of deep canyons in South America, of remote islands, of the Eskimos safe in their Arctic vastness, of humanity ready to start cultural evolution all over again. We were up against the inability to believe in absolute destruction and up against the traditionalism of the military and diplomats bred in ideas formed before 1914. As the iron curtain fell, ideas of overkill prevailed—if they have enough bombs to destroy us *x* times, we must have enough more to destroy them *x* plus two or three or four times.

While the grim arithmetic of deterrence was developing, those of us who were trying to understand what had happened calculated that if we had twenty years without a nuclear war we might make it. In twenty years those who had grown to adulthood beneath the shadow of the bomb would have learned to understand it. They would still be young, too young to occupy positions of power or influence; there would be no generals or presidents or dictators among them. But they would be old enough to ask the right questions; for example, to ask, "After a city has been destroyed, of what use will the weapons be that are designed to destroy it several times more?" This expectation was a precursor of the Generation Gap of the 1960s.

But we had to get through those twenty years, and this would require a supporting climate of opinion. How were we to get groups of human beings to realize what it was they were trying to prevent happening, to realize acutely enough to act, but not so acutely that they would be paralyzed into total denial? Then we phrased it as primarily the difficulty of dramatizing the nature of the new dangers that faced us on earth. I found that those reared on apocalyptic fears of the Last Day could encompass and even enjoy the notion of the total destruction of a sinful world. But those who had been reared in a diluted atmosphere in which there was still a possibility of heaven, but no longer a belief in hell, had no resources for facing total catastrophe. It was a period when children were shielded from the knowledge of death and funeral practices denied the dissolution of the body. The papal decree proclaiming the Assumption of the Virgin Mary to be official Church dogma in 1950 stood as an attempt to combat ideas which denied the resurrection of the body and immortality. From the old peace movements there came equally absolutist expectations of a day when the lion would lie down with the lamb. Lectures which advertised either a discussion of nuclear power or of the Soviet Union were poorly attended.

But the first intimations that perhaps we had been right in expecting new questions came when in the late 1950s young people began to complain of the ideas of their elders. "They seem to believe we can get rid of the bomb. They don't understand that we have to learn to live with it." While their elders were treating the dismantling of atomic bombs as if it were as simple as the disarmament of Germany had been or the scrapping of battleships by the big powers in the 1930s, which succeeded only in building new kinds of Maginot Lines, young people were beginning to recognize that the knowledge of the bomb would be with us into the farthest foreseeable future.

War had become, for the first time in human history, an activity in which everyone would lose everything. But human beings who have been schooled to face desperate odds through the millennia of our existence have learned to survive by forgetting pain and hoping against hope. As the new generation was growing up, the nuclear debate went on and the predictions of the inevitability of an atomic accident did not come true; one after another unpredicted event blunted our fears and thus our ability to take advantage of the first opportunity in history for preventing war.

We domesticated the nuclear bomb; we became obsessed with bases for planes from which it could be launched and underground "silos" where nuclear-armed missiles could be protected. In 1966 a hydrogen bomb was lost after two U. S. Air Force planes collided off the coast of Spain and an American ambassador went swimming with it. Three years before a "hot line" had been established between Moscow and Washington to reduce the danger that the world would be destroyed by bombs automatically let loose because of unexplained blips seen on a radar screen.

Now, in the 1970s, instead of becoming the responsible guardian of world peace, the United States, its allies, and its adversaries all participate actively in the irresponsible and competitive merchandising of arms, nuclear-energy plants, and weapon-quality nuclear materials. Where the atomic bomb presented a clear-cut possibility for deterrence and the partial reassurance of control, the proliferation of commercially used plutonium today presents a kind of danger so diffuse, so unmanageable, that the nightmares of the British novelist Nevil Shute's *On The Beach,* published in 1957, become again a believable depiction of ultimate catastrophe.

But what do the dangers of nuclear power in the late 1970s have to do with the Generation Gap? Ten years ago the Generation Gap could be stated as clearly and simply as the atomic dilemma in the summer of 1945. An unprecedented situation had arisen. As the world became one intercommunicating whole, the experience of all those, everywhere on earth, reared in the post-World War II world, became a shared experience and differentiated them from all their elders. The colleges and universities had exploded under the pressure of their fresh vision. Empowered by this freshness and by the new ethics of shared responsibility, sufficiently alienated from the Establishment—from all establishments—the postwar generation demanded a changed world. It demanded this as surely as the prewar generation's recognition of the bomb demanded a changed world in 1945. The new generation was in fact, the product of the twenty years of grace we had asked for in 1945 when the first atomic explosions changed the world forever.

The Generation Gap, as it occurred in the mid 1960s was both a historical event irreversible in time and a biological event, as it occurred to human beings who would inevitably age. Placed against the background of all known history of *Homo sapiens* on this planet, it was a unique event and could not be expected to happen again. The uniqueness lay in its simultaneity. In previous periods there had been events of equal significance, like the discovery of how to conserve, and later how to make fire, how to make weapons to kill at a distance—the arrow and the dart—how to breed animals and to plant seeds, how to put speech into script and to organize large groups of people into interdependent urban communities. Later, human beings learned how to ask questions that could be answered by disciplined shared observation and experiment, with the resulting technological power that science has given over transportation, communication, the release of energy, the exploration of space, and the medical revolutions which have given us the population explosion, the emancipation of men and women from lifelong parenthood, and a greatly extended life expectancy for both men and women.

The impact of all of these major changes in human cultural evolution came slowly; it took thousands of years for small inventions in stone tools to travel very short distances. Only small parts of the earth's population were affected at one time, and there was no time when all of the earth's people were in communication with each other. Five hundred years ago Europe could have been destroyed without a ripple of effect among the high cultures of the New World, safe until the arrival of the Spanish conquistadors with their superior weaponry.

But with the explorations and inventions of the 1940s, the world did become one, each people subject to the actions of other peoples; a plague developed in one part could now spread to the whole, and all were now exposed to the dangers of total nuclear catastrophe.

In hailing the Generation Gap of the mid-1960s as a moment of opportunity, a moment that would never recur in quite this form again, I was in a sense repeating the response of those of us who were early concerned about the bomb. I was proclaiming that the Generation Gap, tragic as it was for the isolated older generation, frightening as it was to the young who must work without models, nevertheless gave us a unique opportunity to face change in a new way. I realized, of course, that each year the Gap would involve a fresh break between different ages—as the old died off, a new host of infants were born and those who were then disturbing our universities became adults. This meant, and that was clear enough, that the proportions would change each year, until all of those who had been reared before the mid-forties finally died and the unique gap would disappear. During this period, before that happened, while the older generation still held the reins, I and many others hoped we might develop new forms of communication between young and old which would become models for future generations. There would, of course, continue to be vast changes to adjust to. But, we hoped children reared on the other side of the Generation Gap would have an understanding of change which would differ quantitatively and qualitatively from that of their elders. When young people asked, "Will we be as alienated from our children as we are from our parents?" I answered, "I don't think so. There will be no such world-wide gap which will include everyone at once. Change will probably again be more piecemeal, some parts of the world will change at different speeds, and during the present crisis you can learn enough about change itself to be able to bring up children who are really ready for change."

When people had asked questions about what kind of communication we could establish across the Gap and asked how I found it possible to understand what was being said, I had pointed to two circumstances in my own life—the way I had been reared and the discipline of anthropology, where one learns to listen across thousands of years of technological distance. It was when I realized that the anthropological experience itself was too special to provide recommendations which would be of much use to the vast majority of the present generation, as neither they themselves nor their children would be anthropologists, that I decided to write my autobiography *Blackberry Winter*, as a record of how children could be brought up, conscious of the changes which their forebears had undergone, treated as persons with immediate contributions to make, rather than merely as learners not yet deserving of notice. As a childhood friend said to me fifty years later, "In my own house I was a child; in your parents' house I was a person."

There was primarily hope in the 1960s, not that the young would change the world overnight, as they themselves hoped to do, but that the need to include them and their insights would alter our own. Would not the extraordinary degree of separation between generations have effects that could be used constructively? Could we get rid of the belief that to understand others, one had to put oneself in their shoes, often the very worst way of understanding others? Looking at young people all over the world, it was possible for one to ask, "Could not the new kind of solidarity, based on the uniqueness of their shared experience, a solidarity communicated by music more than words, be the basis for new understanding of the differences among them as well?"

In the 1960s we were also witnessing the explosive change that came with the acceptance of the idea that there were other high religions besides Judeo-Christianity and that all the peoples of the world, physically differentiated into what are called "races," were equally capable of learning and using what other peoples of different physiques had invented or discovered. Prejudices were being stripped away. Would it not be possible to use the explicitness of the Generation Gap to go even further than the great religious and ideological systems which have swept the world since time immemorial to form the basis of ever-widening communication with partially shared values?

This was the hope at the end of the 1960s, expressed in many contradictory ways. It was expressed in the flaming belief that the irresponsible consumer society would disappear. This was the hope that the young, the promising gifted young, the cream of their generation, would stem the inevitable dulling and bureaucratizing of the first revolutionary generation in Communist China. This was the hope, expressed very differently, by those Japanese industrialists who recruited future executives from among the most forceful young insurgents.

In the universities, it was the hope of those staff members who knew how moribund and inadequate our university systems had become, as professors droned out their notes, year after year, as if printing had indeed never been invented. It was the hope of those who realized how many of our high schools had become prisons just to keep teen-agers off the streets and our elementary schools places where imagination was stifled but necessary skills no longer learned. The mature members of the older generation realized, differently but often as acutely, the deficiencies and inadequacies and injustices of the societies that had developed in ramshackle, unthinking fashion during the industrial revolution. In the fresh accusing eyes of the young, they saw reflected their own doubts and uncertainties and repudiations. And so all over the world there were strange and sudden capitulations by the perceptive, responsible, and concerned elders, as well as angry, often vicious reactions from those who felt that the very essence of all they held dear was being completely destroyed.

The hopes and the fears were equally extreme. The aftermath has been excessive also. The press decided in the summer of 1970 that the youth movement was over; this again was not a planned campaign of destruction, but born of disappointed hopes when the announcement came from the Nixon White House that nothing the young, or those who sympathized with their aspirations, could do or say would influence the President in any way. Even those college presidents, who had shared the hope of the young, were not received in Washington. And the American media had begun to exploit—and destroy—the more vocal and picturesque of young "leaders" extracted from a movement that was trying to escape from conspicuously fragmented leadership into groping and temporary consensus.

But something else was happening, something that we had allowed for intellectually, but for which no complete provision had been made in our thinking. We knew that the position of the Generation Gap would move up each year, with one more age group included on the other side. But it was not until the gap between the prewar and postwar generations began to appear, not only among the students but among the teachers, that the full implications were clear. The first harbinger came in 1970 with teaching assistants who struck, not as students against the Establishment, but as junior members of the faculty. Where only a few years before, all faculty were on the other side, now the Gap was *inside* the faculty group—young and weak as the members of the new generation were.

The Gap also began to appear at the same time among the teachers in the secondary schools; lines were drawn across the meager little staff rooms where school teachers gathered —the young, bearded evaders of military service in the loathed Vietnam War on one side of the room, the patriotic past-draft-agers on the other. And local school boards, forgetting, with everyone else, that people age a year every year, passed ordinances against ever again employing "young teachers." The slogan "Never trust anyone over twenty-five" was hastily amended to "Never trust anyone over thirty." The "sideburn generation," those whose experience had straddled the Gap, who served both to interpret and to blur the sharpness of the Gap, began to adopt the behavior which had characterized the new generation—their music, their dress, their drugs—and so pave the way for the steady co-op-

tion of the insignia of the new generation by their elders—
scraggy locks framing lined faces, bright-colored waistcoats
spanning too ample waists.

Steadily, the Gap appeared in professional schools, then in
the first years of professional practice. Those organizations
who had set their faces sternly against the wicked nonsense of
the young found even the young people whom they had welcomed because of their short hair, collars and ties, and orthodox manners expressed the same ideas that they had associated with long hair and no ties. Priests who set
themselves against all the new libertarians were likely to find
that the young actors who played the mystery play, *The
Juggler of Notre Dame* were, after all, the young rebels who
had once gathered on the street corner. As I went from campus to campus in the United States, from the most radical to
the least, I encountered applause and laughter at the same
points.

As the first generation of American college students who
had tried to solve the problems of the world by demonstrations in deans' offices or in the streets of Washington left
the campuses and became the first generations in older age
groups—in law schools, medical schools, and business schools
—the intensity of conflicts on the campuses faded. Students,
no longer feeling the full burden of change resting on their
pioneer shoulders, were relieved by the end of the Vietnam
War in April 1975 from the ever present problems of the
draft and decisions of conscience. But they now came under
new and unfamiliar pressures as an economic recession
deepened and the proportionate number of younger students
shrank. Jobs became scarcer because there were so many
more contemporary contenders. It became harder than ever
to get into medical schools and law schools. The grim business of making a living intruded for the first time on the children of the upper middle class who had felt free to choose
whatever course they wished, assured that there would always be money enough.

So the students of the country in the 1970s buckled down

to work again, to the unsatisfactory and outmoded methods of learning, once so recently repudiated, now again to be endured. The urgency their predecessors had felt in the mid-sixties has almost completely gone. Activists are almost as rare as they have traditionally been on American campuses. Undergraduate life is again seen as a perpetuation of adolescence, a postponement of choice, or where a professional choice has been made, for a determined pursuit of its academic requirements. Saving the world, like earning a living, can be postponed until later—when once out of law school, one can take up advocacy or out of medical school, one can work for free clinics. Later, the concerned can go to Washington and get jobs in the Environmental Protection Agency, or join Ralph Nader's crusaders, or go to work overseas in a Peace Corps that is today much more sober and more demanding of skill. The new graduates will not retire to the suburbs any more than their predecessors did. The campuses look more like the 1950s, but the questioning generated on the campuses of the 1960s is still with us.

In the 1960s I found that the fifteen-year-old cry of responsibility articulated by Shannon Dickson of Texas expressed all the poignancy of that first generation faced with a world they never made. In writing the new part of this book, I sought out Shannon Dickson again to see if the way he felt now was an equally significant expression of these older young people in the 1970s. This is what he wrote:

Ten years ago I wrote an essay describing the way much of my generation viewed the world and our relationship to it. At that time, as we began to focus on the larger world beyond the sphere of family and friends, the stark contrast between how we perceived the world and how we felt it should be dominated our awareness. This insight created in us a deep conviction that we must correct the gross inequities in all areas of life and never make the same short-sighted mistakes of our predecessors.

In the late sixties our strong convictions were accompa-

nied by a naïve impatience, born of the "instant satis-
faction" environment in which we were raised, that led us
to believe we could change the world overnight by simply
demanding it. This illusion was shattered in the direct
conflict of our ideals with the complex interactions of these
global problems; so too was the visible display of our
collective emotions quietly transformed into a personal
conflict of molding these ideals into successful and fulfilling
individual lives.

Our methodology of change has certainly been humbled,
yet as we move closer to the nerve centers of government,
education, and business, our original commitments have
become richer and more profound in the realization that
the ball is moving swiftly into our hands and with it the
possibilities of a new and better world. A major difficulty
we find now is that by entering the "accepted" fabric of society, we also are entering career paths laid down by our
elders to achieve their ideals of success and fulfillment
which in many ways are vastly different than ours.

We, the inheriting generation, must alter this course and
be honest with ourselves and our convictions of where we
can take the world. For if we, as individuals, give in to
the expectations of a past that is not ours, then the survival
of our unique species may indeed be short.

CHAPTER SIX

Unanticipated Reverberations of the Generation Gap

Those who were young in the mid-1960s have influenced the world, but it has been a quieter, less continuous, more indirect influence than they or their sympathetic elders hoped. Once there are older young people on the same side of the Generation Gap—young teachers, young doctors, young lawyers, young politicians—it is not necessary for students in their mid-teens to feel they and they alone have to save the world. But the difference that ten years has made is not clear, either to those who were the first generation to look with fresh, appalled eyes at a world they never made or to the students who have come after them, and who worriedly ask themselves whether or not they are apathetic. The speed of change has bemused both, and they both are quick to see superficial differences and forget similarities. Those Western youths who wander to the far corners of the world still sing the same music to each other, but the big gatherings like that at Woodstock in 1970 have disappeared amid the organized hostility of the reactive adult world.

Instead of a simple linear sequence in which the Generation Gap moved in an orderly fashion up the biological progression until all those on the pre-war side were dead, there have been enormous complications. Parents faced their unpredictably and inexplicably alienated children; teachers felt the better they taught the more repudiated they had been; and those who had given their lives to some piece of good works found themselves rejected by the patients, pupils, clients or parishioners whom they had so selflessly served. The ranks of those who hated and feared both the young and everyone who looked young had grown rapidly, as TV showed, day after day, the tiny per cent of student activists battling police somewhere in the world. The opposition to activism had drawn on many sources. There were the millions of members of the new middle class, just arrived by hard work and saving, who had hoped to send their children to colleges from which they would emerge with the credentials for successful upward mobility. There were the police who did not believe in using "bad language" in the presence of ladies, who had to face the provocation of extraordinarily unladylike behavior by the female students from colleges where they had hoped to send their daughters. There were those in middle-management who had reached an upper limit and were holding on by sheer inertia, who were being replaced by the new computer techniques in which the young excelled. There were the farmers whose crops were trampled at the song fests and the farmers who were affronted by young urbanites living in communes who left the cattle standing, in stables, deep in muck. There were the hard-working taxpayers who watched young people from comfortable homes living on food stamps. There were disappointed minorities— black, Spanish-speakers, Native Americans—who had felt that the partisanship the privileged, young upper middle class had shown during the civil rights movement in the 1950s and 1960s had been insincere, self-indulgent, and fleeting.

There were women, newly released from compulsory motherhood, uncertain of the next step. And there were the swelling numbers of the elderly, resentful of having been laid aside, ready to set aside in their turn, disliking the sound of children's voices, the racket of electronically amplified music, the manners and morals of the young. There were the soured middle-aged, brought up in a stricter era, continually titillated and tempted by the flaunted sexuality of the young, culminating in a recent case in which a judge pronounced the rape of a female high school student by a male student as natural, considering the way "girls" dressed nowadays.

There came to be more and more reasons for the embittered elders to fear the streets; they were afraid of attack, afraid of burglary; they were tempted or affronted by both the seductiveness of young males with long "feminine" tresses and young boys and girls with Afro hair-dos looking like aggressive wild creatures ready for battle. Indoors, afraid of the streets, they watch TV, as they watched it in the 1960s, where every sort of crime and excess are enacted before their eyes. They sit immobile, without a muscle stirring to rescue the murdered or the raped. In past periods of our history, the pamphleteers and the novelists of revolt stirred the sympathies of millions, as they read of the horrors of Dickens' workhouses, of Eva and Uncle Tom and southern slavery, of the vicissitudes of the despised, the hunted, and the oppressed. But the TV watcher does not participate as a reader does; the immobilization of the watcher's muscles also immobilizes human sympathy, until a real murder enacted before watching eyes becomes as unreal as a fictional one.

Meanwhile, crimes are being committed by younger and younger adolescents, just as increasing sophistication has handed over to the young many other tasks once reserved for adults. State by state, our laws and our practices have failed to keep up with the changes. Young people may be of an age to vote, but not to decide that their tonsils can be taken out, to conceive but not to have an abortion, to fly in bomber crews that may destroy a city but not to buy a glass of beer. And the numbers of homeless children, doorstep children, teen-agers for whom no adult is really responsible, and runaways, mostly girls in their early teens, have swollen to millions in the United States alone. Such children are indeed dangerous. They have appeared before, often after wars, like the wild children of the U.S.S.R. who became candidates for members of the secret police, bound in love to no one, never having known the binding power of parental love and care. Most children feel murderous at times because of the restrictions imposed by parents, but their aggression is "bound" because they also experience continuous care from the same adults. Today, there are now millions of such unloved children loose in a society in which they see no hope of ever attaining the stark material ambitions encouraged by TV, who see all the old as their enemies. The fear of attack that the old feel is not merely a paranoid reflection of the hostility they themselves feel, but a very real danger. And the powerful old are expressing themselves in a hundred ways: in court decisions that would put youthful converts of proselytizing Asian religions back in the custody of their parents; in closing clinics, stripping schools of every ameliorating new addition, punishing the teachers who rebel for better conditions, crowding the school rooms, closing down children's services —tolerating a new and terrible pornographic exploitation of young children.

The so widely publicized and varied excesses of the young have had wide repercussions throughout society, and many people in the United States, far from concentrating on the well-being of their children, have turned against our children. The situation is not made the more intelligible, when those who fight for the embryo's right to life also advocate capital punishment and the continuation of wars in which napalm is poured on babies.

So as in the case of the possibilities offered by the atomic bomb, the hopes engendered by the Generation Gap and its concomitants have become strangely diffused and blurred. The young have been put on university boards of trustees, but in ways that make little difference—and for the most part leave them bored. If the good effects have sometimes seemed to run throughout the veins of society like a tonic, the ill effects, the reactivity, the hostility, the reinforced rejection of change, have spread like a metastasized cancer. Each effect is harder to identify, harder to deal with. Hope is much harder to come by today than it was ten years ago. When the first members of the new generation entered the lists, they believed that the members of the Establishment were in charge—mistaken, but in a powerful position that could be challenged. Today, it is becoming only too obvious that nobody is in charge. The grounds for hope and action on nuclear dangers looked simple in 1945 and desperately complicated today. The grounds for hope in the mid-1960s, as a fresh-eyed generation supported Eugene McCarthy in the New Hampshire presidential primaries and came home again to what looked like a possible world, are also much more confused today.

The whole picture is made the more confusing because we have returned to the point at which the change was perceived as just a conflict between adolescents and parents in the 1960s. It took some time to realize that this was no ordinary battle between disapproving parents and dissident children, but included also all older people, all relationships between all the young and all their elders. Today, it is again adolescents and parents of adolescents who are still, in all cases, looking at each other across the Generation Gap. There are young teachers, young doctors, and the parents of young children on the same side of the Gap as the adolescents. But nowhere in the world are there adolescents whose parents are not on the other side of the Gap. In New York and London, in Cincinnati and Rome, in Moscow and Tokyo, among Eskimo and among the peoples of Papua New Guinea, parents and children face each other across the Gap. As the significance of the Gap has been blurred by the changes of the last ten years, again young adult models are available to students and apprentices, and the persistence of the Gap between parents and children becomes all the more striking. It is this that gives a continuing poignancy to parenthood in the 1970s, as it did to all adulthood in the 1960s. This is still the hardest time that the world has ever known to have adolescent children or to be an adolescent.

Meanwhile, many older people continue to expect the Gap to be where it was, in the late teen-age group and on the college campuses. Their erstwhile sympathizers lament the loss of activism, berate young people for having somehow sold out —as a few of the more conspicuous and exhibitionistic of their precursors certainly have. And the turbulent relationships between adolescents and parents continue, although the Gap itself is now in the late twenties age group, and many of the new generation have children of their own. But within the family, the conflicts between young people and parents continue, blurred somewhat by the turbulent years on the campuses having died down. High school students speak of their parents as having "learned a lot," and parents, especially upper-middle-class parents, now often try to outdo each other in describing the curious behavior of their children, who are living in "arrangements," trying to grow food without pesticides, turning to handicrafts, or currently, to the cultivation of mystical experience.

As the original Generation Gap is less conspicuous, and the lines between old teachers and young teachers, young politicians and old politicians, young doctors and old doctors are less sharply drawn, the fact that the Gap still exists between all adolescents and their parents is being again perceived as just a familiar generational change or an ordinary generational conflict, characterized by the particularities of the present period in history. Those professors and teachers who encountered the Gap originally between themselves and young people in their late teens, sigh with relief as their present-day students, supported by the existence of their older brothers and sisters out in the world, are less difficult to teach and to talk to. But parents who encounter adolescent children for the first time, still experience much of the same alienation between generations that gave its name to the Generation Gap. It was only when the break appeared at universities all over the world that it was realized that this wasn't simply a normal parent-child conflict. Now that it doesn't exist at the universities and there are so many adults on the same side of the Gap as adolescents, it again looks to many adolescents and their parents like their own particular conflict. It is possible that some of the resentment of the young can be allayed if they can place their trials and tribulations in a wider context, and that some of the guilt and despair of the parents can be allayed if they realize that their children are reacting not only to them, as particular parents, but within a context in which they, unlike the new parents of small children, are still experiencing the Generation Gap in all its poignancy.

Yet in a great majority of homes, parents and adolescents have taken a stance that makes no allowance for this wider conflict. So, in the essays of college freshmen about the Generation Gap, only an occasional student discusses adolescent behavior as symbolic rather than personal. In 1977 Donald E. Sparks, a freshman, wrote:

Many styles of clothing and personal appearance of today's youth set them apart from their parents and other middle-aged people. The youth of today wear anything that is still holding together not because they have to but because of their own personal taste. In a way this irritates the older generation because they remember when they had to wear hand-me-downs. Being more extreme and able to maintain their own standards, today's youth are alienated by the middle-class, middle-aged working force. The hair on teenage men is one of the surest points of alienation. . . . I feel that today's youth are trying new experiments by challenging the length of hair. . . . Hair can be controlled by the youth without having to use a highly informative computer. . . . [Hair] to some youth is a means to experiment and be different, while to others it is a way to challenge and go against the system of the middle-aged.

The middle-aged people not liking long hair have tried some very clever and tricky maneuvers in the past to do away with this problem. Not until approximately three years ago did schools allow long hair on their students. The schools whose sole job was supposed to be to teach and not set moral standards for their students didn't stay with that. The schools of today believe they should help bring the youth up the right way, their way. If you didn't like their way and went against it, they would say they have no other choice but [to] punish the disorderly stu-

dent. Many a time they would expel students from my
school due to the length of the students hair. The funny
thing is that when the dress code for hair was dropped everything went on the same old way. What I am trying to
say is that the length of an individual's hair does in no way
supply a mental shade or block to the advancement of
learning.

What danger is in the length of hair any individual
chooses? Many dangers lie in that particular item. It seems
that when someone can't do what he wants to because
someone else is telling him that it's wrong, the person who
supposedly is wrong is immediately on the offense wanting
to get back. Many parents tell their teenage boys that they
look like girls with long hair. This is a bad scene because
the kid then doesn't know if he can really talk to his parents or not. Many say that a lack of communications causes
a generation gap. I feel that in the case of hair not only is
there a lack of communications but mainly a lack of understanding. But, there is still hope. Many of today's middle-
aged are allowing a few more inches on the top side.

But a much larger group sounds more like high school students with the goals of the 1950s clashing with old-fashioned
parents who can be classified as "depression-era children" by
a student like Jim Stein:

> There is a large gap between the way I think and the
> way my parents think about values today:
> My parents and I differ in opinion on many things, but
> there are certain subjects we really are far apart on: music,
> cars, and money. These three topics constitute a major part
> of the generation gap in our home. My views on these are
> almost totally opposite to those of my parents. There is a
> large gap between the way I think and the way my parents
> think of values today.
> On the subject of money, my parents (depression-era
> children) feel that money should be saved to buy or spend
> on things of importance. I feel this way too, but that is

where the similarity ends. The things my parents feel are important are limited to a college education, insurance, and a house. I admit each one is very important for the future, but I am living right now too. This is an important part of my life. I want to travel a lot. See things I will not have a chance to see when I am burdened with paying for a house, insurance etc. Travelling and experiencing new things is something I will never forget, or regret. Most older people tell me to "do it now while you are still young," and that is what I want. My parents feel it is useful to a certain extent but not to be done very often. Other items I like to spend money on, like stereo equipment, guns, etc., are also looked down upon by my parents. They feel it is needless to spend larger amounts of money ($200 or over) on this type of thing because the money should be put to better use, i.e., the aforementioned house and insurance. Guns and stereo equipment are "merely a phase I am going through," they say. Nonetheless, I earned the money and feel I should be the one who determines how it is to be spent.

Automobiles is another subject on which my parents and I differ. I like "sporty" cars that look nice and run fairly fast. They like small economy cars. My mom is trying to get me to buy a Volkswagen, while I want something like a Camaro. I feel it is worth the added cost of insurance and gas to have a sporty looking car. My parents think a car is just a car and does not have to look good. I contend that with as much time as I spend in my car going to school and work, it should be something I enjoy driving. I feel that since it is my car, I should have the choice.

Music is a subject my parents and I might never agree on. My parents like music by the big bands like Glenn Miller's, or country and western by artists like Johnny Cash. Believe it or not, I like that music also. The discrepancy comes in with "acid rock" musicians such as the late Jimi Hendrix, Led Zeppelin, Foghat, etc. I enjoy listening to fast paced music with a lot of volume. The music and the volume prove to be too much for mom & dad. They cannot seem to understand why anyone would want to listen to that "noise." I cannot effectively explain the reasons to them. I just let it go as something we will never see eye to eye on.

There is definitely a generation gap in my family. My parents are conservative in their thinking, partly because of the depression. They feel that a secure future is more important than fun and games now. I, however, feel that the age I am at now is important. I feel I should do the things now that I will not have a chance to do later. I believe that life is to be enjoyed. A person should not be a slave of the future. The future is important, but not important enough to waste today.

Or this comment by Pat Overby:

My parents' idea of what a car is for is in complete contrast to my uses for a car. . . .

In particular, my parents had a negative attitude from the outset when I announced that I was acquiring for myself a good-looking Camaro that they would qualify as a "hot rod." I fell in love with the car and take exceptional care of it. Of course, according to my parents a car is for taking the driver from point A to point B. Any other aspects of that car, such as the way it looks or sounds, are superfluous. My contention, however, is that if a car can make driving a pleasure rather than a necessity, it should be so.

Whereas an automobile's primary function is transportation, I believe it should be more, at least for those who desire it. My car has a bright new paint job, new rubber and wheels, and a fifteen-hundred-dollar engine, but that is how I like it, and this should not be a matter of concern for my parents. It is true that my parents use their car only as a means of getting around town, but in my case I have attached a certain stratified feeling to my own auto. I enjoy cruising around the town in my car, showing it off, and driving just to relax my mind. Obviously, this is not the intention my parents have of putting their car to use.

Certainly my parents make clear their feelings about my car. Yet there is one point they fail to consider. My car is more than a means of transportation. It provides me and my friends with a hobby that we enjoy working on. However, my father views my car only as an expensive toy. I sometimes wonder if he has forgotten the times in his teens that he spent fooling around with cars, tinkering around with the engine, even if only to see what made it work. I am well satisfied with my car, and I respect my parents' view about it. As long as I have this car and am living with my parents, it will continue to broaden the generation gap in our house.

The expressions of the Generation Gap in the 1960s were perceived as part of larger social movements—civil rights in the United States, the struggle against the Vietnam War, the Algerian independence movement against France, or the struggles in Cyprus, the effort of young people to introduce a new honesty about sex and new attitudes toward the human body. But today, as the intensity of the generational conflict has been perpetuated most markedly within the family, there is a tendency to blame disorganization within the family itself as a principal cause of symptoms such as delinquents running away from home, teen-age drug taking, and teen-age alcoholism. And perhaps even more striking are the retreat of high school students from identifying the conditions of conflict in the wider community and the divergent social goals and standards between elders and young people to a demand for a new spiritual context. Not only has the international Club of Rome shifted its attention, from calling for limits to growth economically and ecologically, to a search for values, but this new emphasis is permeating society and providing new content for generational alienation.

CHAPTER SEVEN

New Forms of Commitment

In my first formulations of the Generation Gap, when I conjured up a picture of the future which could be shared—because like a conceived but unborn child, it was unknown—it made a fine climax. It seemed like a solution to many of our problems. As peoples all over the world came into the modern world at the same time, it was very tempting to offer a model that could let them all start afresh. Whether they came in at Gate 1, or Gate 23, or Gate 2003—if we visualize the modern world as a vast airport, into which planes entered from different distances and directions—they all responded to the same voice from the control tower, all moving toward the same unknown future.

I pictured what had happened in the mountains of New Guinea, as naked, aspiring men, who had washed the pig fat out of their hair, arrived at a government post saying, "We have built a school and hospital. Please send us a doctor and a teacher"—calling for emissaries of that modern world they had heard about and craved to enter. And the picture is true, in the sense that this is what really happened and is happening all over the world. People who have only seen airplanes in the sky and heard of the wonderful ways of radio, satellites, telescopes, microscopes, engines, and script are eager to experience these marvels for themselves. And given the individual ability and the belief that he can learn, the son of a New Guinea head-hunter can learn calculus as well as the boy whose forebears have been engineers in a North German harbor town for generations or the Cretan peasant whose ancient forebears developed a unique civilization four thousand years ago. What any group of human beings has learned, the members of every other group, each according to his individual abilities, can learn also. Those eager or blasé children around the world, some bright-eyed in leaf-roofed huts, some crowded together on rough schoolroom benches, some dozing, bored in the plastic wonders of expensive secondary schools in American suburbs—are all entering the same world, a world their parents never knew as children. And they do share the same experience of watching satellites in the sky above their heads and of coming to think of them as everyday events so that fourteen-year-old American children speak of being interested in space when they were young and fourteen-year-old New Guinea children map their villages as they must look from the sputnik.

They do have in common a childhood that none of their parents anywhere in the world experienced and they can look forward to a shared future, for never again will they be completely cut off from the rest of the world for longer than the duration of a hurricane, a power failure, or a political coup. Mathematicians and physicists and chemists from Japan and China, India and Soviet Russia, America and Sri Lanka and Tanzania, can communicate through diagrams on a blackboard without interpreters, although it is still doubtful whether they can share a single formal meal together without being categorized as hopelessly alien, boorish, uneducated, or downright unfriendly. The cultures from which they come span the last twenty thousand years of human cultural evolution, and the differences in the way their parents and elders see the world are so complex that it takes many years of very hard study for scholars and scientists from one culture to learn enough about another one to understand it at all. So we must still come to terms in the shared world of the future on the basis of pasts that are incomparably different. Yet one of the ways in which human pasts are not so different is in our common biological base; we are all born of women, fed at women's breasts or from their plastic substitutes from which we nevertheless must suck for sustenance. We all have to learn to walk and talk; to grasp what we reach for; to laugh and cry, not when we would, but when it is appropriate; to feel hungry at the correct time and sleepy when tradition says sleep is in order. And we all share the process of maturation and aging, and for all of us this is a one-way process, proceeding inexorably from birth to death, however differently poets and religious dogma may phrase it. This is so, whether infants are thought of as reincarnations of their great-grandparents or quite newly made, leaping in their mothers' wombs as life is felt; whether old age is equated with a second childhood or with the ultimate outcome of a single lifetime or equated with the end of a half-circle, with infant and old age closer to heaven and middle-age a nadir farthest from the heaven to which human souls recurrently return. But these beliefs inform and transform the lives we lead until they are in many respects almost unrecognizable as equally intelligible and equally human. Beliefs may even change the rhythm, so that in some cultures the young never learn anything new after the age of seven or eight and in others an oldster with a fine tremor may learn a new skill. Among the Abkasians of the Caucasus, where old age does not require the cessation of any activities, ninety-year-olds work and dance, make love and sing, as they did when they were young, in a pattern shrunken only in amplitude, with two hours of work where once they worked twelve, and everything else done proportionately more lightly.

In Euro-American everyday expectations of life and in our religious beliefs, those of us who have been reared within the heritage of Greece and Rome and Judeo-Christianity—with our traditions neatly preserved in a script that is linear and phonetic and a common religious belief that each human being has but one life to live—have come to think in almost exclusively linear terms. The future lies ahead, the past behind, the present is all around us. For the unlettered peasant and, at a deep level, for the child who had been cared for by an unlettered peasant nurse the world retains some of the circularity of the repetitive natural cycle of planting and harvesting and the phases of the moon, but for most of us, the linearity of our whole script-ridden heritage took over. We habitually see the past as effecting or causing the future.

The Generation Gap, as a particular break between the experience of those who grew up at one period of time and that of those who grew up after the changes of the mid-1940s, is congruent with the kind of thinking which is so deeply engrained in our approach to life. In the United States we have been the more prepared to accept the Gap by generations in which immigrants reared in other cultures have come here, superficially adapted and died, leaving their children, Americans by upbringing, behind them. We are accustomed to the second-generation comment, "We did that till my grandmother died. Then it was over." And so often the American-born children refused to learn grandmother's language—often it was an unwritten dialect—and learned to speak only American English.

A comparable shedding of the past was one of the characteristics of the first rebellious members of the new generation in the 1960s. Poorly schooled, they were almost doomed to lose in any argument with their elders, so they substituted abusive epithets for discussion, determined to be no longer put down by those who had lived longer and had participated in building an unbearable, unlivable world. Fraternization across the color line, adoption of children of conspicuously different physiques, active refusal to trust anyone over twenty-five, agreement to trust in those who shared the same new experiences, distrust in anyone who did not—these were the standard behaviors.

Under such circumstances, apocalyptic hopes flourished. Were we to have a bright new world, a really brave new world, from which the haunting prophecies of the late George Orwell could be banished and technology shaped to human needs instead of human needs subordinated to technology? Could the Christian message that the "Sabbath was made for man" actually be extended to computers and rocket launching? Even those who disputed the strength of the Generation Gap argued mechanistically and linearly that there were individuals on both sides of the gap who shared certain attitudes and that these shared attitudes, of rebellion or conservatism, were more crucial than the attitudes shared within the opposing generations. But the image of a frozen generation of young people remained strong. They were characterized as lost and expected somehow to retain only the outstanding charactcristics of thcir alicnation or to capitulatc, take well-paying jobs and move to the suburbs.

But as the moon shots multiplied in the 1960s, other things were happening, some remarked, some unremarked. Interest in space, so lively among the young children, was rapidly complemented by an interest in exploration under the sea. Interest in science fiction, which depicted marvelous or monstrous futures, was complemented by an interest in early man and in our prehuman past. To counteract the sense of living all alone, the unwilling custodians of a world they never made, overpowered by an aging Establishment, young people began reaching for anchorage, for roots. The buildings of the present seemed unsteady, likely to topple from inadequate foundations.

The extent to which the world was being weighed down by millions of the old still in power, getting older without losing their power, was not nearly as present in consciousness in the 1960s as it is in the 1970s. The temporary hope of young leadership, who ruled in new countries some fifteen years ago, brightened by the youthful looking President John Kennedy, dwindled as the whole world mourned for him as a symbol of youth destroyed.

We have traveled from a three-generation world, in which grandparents had once been allies of grandchildren in a postfigurative culture, but in the United States had become useless rejected remnants of the past, to the cofigurative culture of the 1960s, when there were often four or even five generations alive. And with four generations, many of the old images toppled also. In the industrialized world, we began to have men and women standing in the middle, responsible for two generations above and two generations below. In the developing world all the efforts of public health were placed on infant and maternal welfare. The middle-aged died, half of the population was under fifteen, and there were not enough elders to carry the load of rearing the children. As prophets of doom began to warn about the population crisis, these two conditions—increased longevity in the affluent world and disproportionate infant survival in the developing world—merged in a common outcry in which human beings were treated as pollution. With the sense of the world's being overcrowded with masses bearing down too heavily on the resources of our crumbling oases and vanishing forests and eroded hillsides, there came a rejection of both the too-many old and the too-many young. There have been cries of life-boat ethics, of triage—demands to let India go down the drain as hopeless, demands for euthanasia and turning off the life-support systems for the hopelessly ill. On the streets of modern cities helpless, tottering, anonymous old people are attacked and murdered, and in their lonely dwellings old women are done to death.

There are, in effect, other by-products of the Generation Gap besides the sense of loneliness of the elderly and the lack of models for the young. Many of the old, whose hands would have been restrained from boxing the ears of their successors by the comforting image of replication of themselves, feel no such restraint when all the young, including their own children have turned into strangers. And the young, still powerless, still struggling in a world the defects of which they see only too clearly, many with parents who wish their children had never been born, feel bitter, anonymous rage against the old. Each enactment of this conflict worsens the situation. A million old people see an account of one murder on TV and shudder when they see a group of youngsters on a street corner. The target of youthful attack fights back and is killed, as the young attackers are trapped between their own ruthlessness and the rage of their victim.

Both young and old see the others too impersonally and therefore too inhumanly. The professor who had spent twenty years teaching responsibly felt repudiated even when students attacked *other* professors who spent all their time off the campuses. He could not grasp that the students who were attacking were not *his* students, and in the end he felt totally repudiated, embittered, unfairly rejected.

So we come to the image of the future, how it can be shared and whether an unborn child, though so appropriate, can suffice as an image in a world in which living children themselves are being repudiated. Perhaps the reason we are having so much difficulty in taking responsibility for the future, as we pile up plutonium wastes to threaten our descendants for thousands of years, is just because our tie with our children was so abruptly and so cruelly broken in the 1960s. The adult world, the world of middle age and power, is like a world of childless property owners who resent the school taxes because they have no children of their own. In a sense, the Generation Gap made the whole world childless. When I first looked at this, my heart was filled with sympathy for parents, realizing that the whole human endeavor has been powered through the ages by parents' willingness to give their lives for their children, women risking themselves over and over in childbirth, men risking themselves in warfare and in dangerous and life-consuming work. But I think I did not reckon heavily enough on the inevitable hostility that would accompany the parents' alienation.

The English anthropologist Geoffrey Gorer has pointed out that true hate is impersonal hate and that it is impossible to hate completely any person whose identity is fully known. But to this I would add that the other condition of true merciless hatred is feeling trapped with the ones who are hated whether they are intimately known or not. The trap may be of various kinds. Murder of husbands or wives is very common when one sees no other way out, because desertion or flight is psychologically or financially impossible. Hatreds mount steadily between two groups that feel boxed in by a third power, like the Protestant and Catholic Irish by the British in Northern Ireland, or two ethnic groups of slum dwellers equally helpless in the same American slum.

The very universality of the Generation Gap became a kind of prison, a prison from which both the young and their elders have been trying to escape. The young wander the world, seeking gurus which the young revere because they come from another culture. But their elders have no people whom they can think of as the old kinds of descendants who replicate themselves, although the elders make frantic attempts to recapture their children from the new missionaries who take advantage of the alienation of the young from their parents. So we now even have an embryonic profession of those who specialize in "kidnapping" alienated children and brainwashing them back from some intrusive Oriental cult.

The sense of alienation is also being incorporated *within* the new generation, as young people in communes refuse to cherish their own children. In *The Children of the Counterculture,* by John Rothchild and Susan Wolf, we find reports of a drama of repeated parental rejection that is hard to interpret without realizing that as new-generation parents themselves have forced their parents to let them go in total repudiation, so they in turn are making comparable demands on their children.

Children were once the sure symbol of continuity and hope, the one certain value which brought all other values into focus. But today, there is a growing ambivalence all around the world, a feeling that there are too many children, too many of the wrong kinds of children—too many affluent children, each of whom is consuming more than his or her share of irreplaceable resources, and too many poor children in poor countries where every gain their countries make is swallowed up by the sheer number of children. So children are becoming a less certain rallying point. Particular children can still call forth dedication, but we need ways for all adults who are not parents to cherish children who are not their own.

Contact between generations is a necessity, but it has been lost in the desperate unplanned helter-skelter of the post-World War II world, as old and young, rich and poor, peoples with more or less racial inheritance from one continent than from another all have been segregated from each other and become explosively miserable without feeling the tempering effects of diversity.

The communes of the 1960s have been succeeded by thousands of less conspicuous experiments, with people living together in small groups, in shorter periods—even more weekends—in workshops, in clusterings; as cults and crafts groups; as producers of little magazines; in new combinations of the handicapped in which the deaf lead the blind. The sturdily stubborn moderate the reckless carelessness of the overimpetuous, and the search for new futures is mixed inextricably with the search for a reassuring past. But we do not have the necessary architecture for all this, the shapes of the new kinds of human habitats. We need houses and towns and cities that will be given form not by the mindless spread of motor transport based on cheap oil and unplanned despoiling of the countryside but by the kind of planning which makes growth possible—sketch maps of the future, in which growth and change, uncommitted space, provision for new ways in which people can relate to each other, will be built not in concrete but in new flexible forms of town planning.

Where the 1960s gave to the world an unreal sense of rapid change, change that could be welcomed with open arms or repudiated with set jaws, the 1970s is a time of scattered experiments, of reported disasters in many parts of the world—of cities that fall to rebellions, of planes hijacked—of New York or London distracted from overwhelming economic distress by "tall ships" or royal coaches. It is like bread dough when it is first mixed and the yeast begins to bubble over the surface, ready to rise, but not yet begun to rise. But such stirrings bring no comfort to those who know nothing of bread making.

Here there will be those who say, "Why are you using such an old figure of speech? No one makes bread anymore, except cranks and housewives with too little to do; it's a feminine image anyway, and the kitchen and everything in it is a symbol of female servitude." But there are life processes which each time they occur have an intrinsic reality—a seed sprouts, a moth emerges from a chrysalis, a leaf falls as it dies. One of our problems today is how to keep the kind of images which have given meaning to human life since human beings found words that could describe something that was not present.

The just-bubbling dough has not begun to rise. We have no picture either of a destroyed Establishment or of a world in which we are certain we want to live. Only a very few would like to make journeys to the moon or spend much time on a space satellite. Only a few more yearn to return to some Eastern religion, from which their Euro-American versions diverged thousands of years ago. Only a few, with other sources of income, want to wrest a living from the earth with tools abandoned long ago. We are indeed still boxed in, unwillingly share as a prison a world which is intercommunicating and interdependent, but of which we are not yet citizens and in which no one is in charge. If we let plutonium proliferate, the United States, the U.S.S.R., and many other countries will be in positions to destroy all life on this planet, but without either the vision, the resources, or the power to save it. This is the dilemma within which so many live troubled lives, vacillating between blind hope and blind despair, in a world that they do not feel they had any part in making and that they can find no way in which they can help to make over.

We are without an image of the future that can rally our loyalties beyond all question of whether anything is worth dying for. We can find many ringing words out of the past, carrying temporary freight of meaning, to set beside Prime Minister Winston Churchill's ringing,

> ". . . we shall fight on the beaches, we shall fight on the landing grounds, we shall fight in the fields and in the streets, we shall fight in the hills; we shall never surrender."
>
> (Speech, House of Commons, June 4, 1940)

But we do not know how to translate such words in a world in which wars cannot be won. What we have to fear today is not—as it was in President Franklin Roosevelt's day—fear itself; instead, we have somehow to rally enough fear so that we can act, but not enough to cause panic or paralysis. The little ships that sailed into the forbidden Pacific waters in the summer of 1973 where the French were about to explode an H-bomb, found a new unity with each other. Indigenous islanders with thousands of years behind them and Europeans newly come as colonists and conquerors to Australia and New Zealand felt for the first time they were fellow citizens in an emerging Pacific comity. But the deed required no deaths, only possible political inconvenience. Turning that small moral armada into something more dangerous would have destroyed the very purpose for which the minor risks were taken; yet the minor risks were good. But who are those who will take the minor risks, risks which may entail some hardship, some sacrifice, a lot of patient, repetitious, inherently boring, definitely unglorious activity? Who will undertake this in a world in which children are reared to expect water to come boiling hot out of a spigot and lights to shine with no more effort than finding and flipping the switch?

We face two new problems: how to remember enough of past pain and disaster so that we can take steps to see that we do not experience such disaster again; and how to be willing enough to die for something valued more than life itself, in a way that will make us willing to live for that same value rather than die. Throughout our human past, the individual capacity to forget pain has made it possible for human beings to build again on the slopes of active volcanoes. Although this capacity to forget those things which would have been intolerable to remember has served us well for millennia, such courage is mere criminal foolhardiness when it means building a hospital or a nuclear plant on a known fault line where there may be an earthquake any day. The willingness of a man to die for the "ashes of his Fathers and the Temples of his Gods" has enabled human beings to build a thousand cities and defend them, for a time, against destruction.

Today these ancient virtues of courage and willingness to die for one's beliefs need to be transmuted: unable to remember pain, we need ectogenetic ways of reminding ourselves of past disaster, cultural landmarks to bolster us against ancient biological capacities. Where no war can be won, warfare cannot be offered as the model of sacrifice. But in some way not fully sensed as yet, it is willingness to lose one's life that makes it possible to find it.

One of the contemporary answers has been to change the nature of commitment from total life-long commitment to limited, provisional types of commitment. In an astonishingly short period of time, the major absolute commitments of Euro-American culture have been transformed, in marriage, in religion, and in politics. "Until death us do part" is a vow that fewer and fewer young people feel they can take. Within monastic orders, final vows are now postponed for many years and a place is made for those who, having made them, cannot, in conscience, keep them. Within institutionalized communism a loss of commitment can be masked in retirement from professionalized political activity.

But we do not yet know how to create a culture in which it will be possible to learn from the past, no matter how painful, and to incorporate a commitment to life which has the strength without the absoluteness of a commitment to death. In some ancient cultures, death of men in battle is equated with death of women in childbirth. But there is one great difference between the way they are expected to risk their lives. For while men are expected to die to protect future generations, women are expected to live and to protect future generations by continuous, unflagging daily care. Perhaps if we build societies in which fathers take as much care of infants and young children as mothers do and feel a child will be equally bereaved if it loses either father or mother, we may find new answers.

CHAPTER EIGHT

Hope Within Technology

In this strangely unheroic age, more individual acts of bravery, of heroism, of dedicated self-sacrifice are performed than ever before, simply because there are more fires into which firemen must plunge, more risks policemen must run, more vigils nurses must stand over burned children, more risks surgeons must take in hours-long operations the very natures of which were undreamed of two decades ago. But none of these efforts add up, not even the courage of a pilot confronting a hijacker, of the single stalwart leader braving a riot, of the smiling candidate for office moving among crowds any one of which may harbor an assassin, of parents who take their defective infant home though it may mean for them a lifetime of self-sacrifice. All of these, we feel, are balanced and possibly nullified by the amount of self-interest, greed, selfish disregard of other people, relentless pursuit of individual gain, lack of conscience in public places, and general lack of higher purpose in the world. Not only industries organized to reap profit in one part of the world in order to wield power in another, but every sort of association and organization, each small church and club designed to benefit some group competes with some other, if not in the market place of profits or political power, then for souls, constituents, prestigious names, or, in the United States, tax-exempt dollars. In a time like the present, of small wars and no big ones, even if it cannot properly be called peace—and it is possible that "war" and "peace" are indeed obsolescent historical terms—the absence of an overarching purpose is matched by the seeming smallness, meaninglessness, and self-centeredness of most peoples' lives. The complaints about loss of direction and purpose and the search for personal involvement seem only to match the deterioration of responsible citizenship and stewardship for community, country, and the life of the world. These are not, unfortunately, "times that try men's souls."

But every decision we make to let a living thing die hardens our heart. Each decision that a society makes consciously to sacrifice any of its members—to let the poor starve, the old drag on in misery, the children go unprotected into epidemic dangers and ignorance—depletes a society's moral resources. Similarly, each act of generosity restores them. It becomes therefore a social task to organize human lives in ways that leave room for shared responsibility. Human beings are seldom capable of total selflessness or total selfishness. Throughout their lives their behavior depends upon the context. The same police may be organized as protectors of the peace or as furies creating the riots they are supposed to prevent. The difference may be only a matter of minutes, of a small crowd out of hand, of a closed space with frightened people pushed against the wall, of a misunderstood order. Within adult personalities, the rapacities of helpless infancy and the overwhelming fear of abandonment exist side by side with patience and a desire to see that their children are treated more gently. Views of human beings which picture them as wholly good or wholly bad obscure the importance of social arrangements and the transformations through which individuals, communities, and nations can go.

If we realize the dangers which accompany an emerging prefigurative period in an overcrowded and intercommunicating world, then we can consciously foster ways of life, consciously pick and choose among technological alternatives, and in the act of doing so, perhaps find the kind of overarching purposes that we seek. The old conundrum "Do we flee because we are frightened or are we frightened because we flee?" still holds. Courage rises when people keep their heads, panic spreads in a crowded enclosure in which any individual fights to reach an exit.

A prefigurative society is by definition a society with an unknown future, and an unknown future is inevitably disconcerting, if not downright frightening. The sense that the children are a little better prepared to face these unknowns because they are at least birthright members of the newer order can be either comforting and give hope or be twisted into a philosophy of despair. But there is a constant danger, more constant than I realized ten years ago, that the struggle will prove too difficult, and the by-products too destructive. Hope for the future must also be balanced, and rooted in memory of the past. Without such deep roots, then shallowly rooted plants, however beautiful the blossoms, will wither in the first drought.

There is another characteristic of hope that has to be remembered: as the Bible says, "Hope deferred maketh the heart sick." One reason why the care of small children is so renewing and heartening that women have been sustained by it all their lives is that a small child learns something new every day—to give an answering smile, to sit up, to reach, to imitate a sound. The nurse or mother can share in the tremendous sense in which each piece of learning, because it is new in the child, seems to be almost like creation itself. Watching children learn is a kind of polar opposite to the planning of the mechanical engineer or of the architect who only puts a human being in his drawings to show the scale. Where one is dealing with totally empty space—a square mile in which every hummock has been leveled and every tree felled to make room for a "development"—the only complement to the destructive emptiness is a blueprint of the "homes" that are to stand there. We have been leveling the ground and cutting down the trees all over the world and putting up great artificial structures, cluttered with functional unrelatedness, like elevator signals which are keyed to the warmth of a human finger and become useless when there is a fire. The new towns, once so inviting in their welcoming spaces, in the invitation to build wisely and well, repel by the very overplanning that should have made them habitable.

Particularly today, when the world is in the hands of those who had to learn to understand it, clumsily, belatedly, and in many ways not at all, we need to introduce processes of growth instead of bulldozing our way through destroyed landscape to ends that prove sterile, disappointing, and ineptly planned. The anthropologist Gregory Bateson has emphasized the destructiveness of linear purposes. The young, in rebellion, have wanted to start from scratch and build their own houses with their own hands, only to find that this also means cutting down trees.

All over the world the distances of the soldier from his enemy and the producer from the consumer have increased; each action has become more impersonal and part of a scale which has got completely out of hand. The nationally based, multinational corporations are frightening just in proportion to the way they are constrained by no immediacy of need or responsibility. Their investments move from shoes to books, from shoelaces to bottle openers, in response to computerized records of profits and losses, and no object that is made is fitted to its best use. In the Middle-West grain growing area of the United States, the deserted unpainted farmhouses stand like ghosts of an age when there were gardens and fowls in the dooryard; the great, bleak, treeless plains, loaded with fertilizer, serviced by machines, produce grain as a factory might produce a product on a conveyor belt, to be sent half a world away. The decision that ends in farmers' cutting down the last trees, planted so desperately during the dust-bowl periods of the depression of the 1930s, are made in the grain markets and the foreign offices of the world, where neither the state of the land nor the need of the starving are taken into account. Where in the villages, men and women together once planted and harvested and kept seeds for the next planting, the progressive centralization of decision has meant the exclusion of one half of that former partnership.

Women no longer take part, left behind in domestic roles, and food is treated either as a weapon or as a counter in the market places of the world.

Wherever we look, we see this process of centralization, of production in one country for use in another of cars and planes, trucks and tractors, tankers and ships, teapots and saucepans, chairs and tables that are designed and shipped to users the designers have never seen. And as late as ten years ago, there seemed no hope of stemming the tide of centralization and dehumanization. Young people went out into empty places and tried to pound grain with unshaped stones, seeking to return to a state that human beings had happily left behind them thousands of years ago. But it was only too obvious that we were not going to feed a world population of four billion with the simple technology of the remote past. Automobiles were still spreading relentlessly, crowding the wide avenues of Nairobi and Moscow and the crooked narrow streets of London and Athens, their owners undeterred by taxes, the price of gasoline, and inconvenience. Prophets lamented the invention of the internal combustion engine, but the whole world, developed and undeveloped, was dominated—up until 1973—by a technology based on cheap oil, rivaled only by the menace of nuclear power.

By the 1970s a few voices were being lifted. Some pointed out that, in fact, the resources did not exist to raise people's standard of living all over the world to the present wasteful level of the industrialized countries. Talk of the Generation Gap was echoed in the talk of a gap between two arbitrarily polarized groups, the rich and the poor countries. The worried advocates of the poor pointed out that if the price of the raw materials, the export of which the poor countries depended on, was raised to give their people a living wage, the rich countries would probably simply turn to manufacturing more synthetics. Wool and rubber and cotton, hemp and wood, would be replaced and the poorer would be poorer than before. And suddenly the world realized that this would also take energy and increase pollution and so we had the beginning of what is now a growing recognition that the way of life, the kind of food production, the kind of transport, the kind of city that burgeoned all over the world since the industrial revolution, is ending. Because cheap oil and everything that went with it is at an end, a disdain for distance, for unnecessary scale, for dehumanization of life, for the destruction of cities, for the glaring contrast between rich and poor, between and within nations, could now be questioned.

It is not, as many people have been led to believe, that technology need control our lives or that we as helpless pawns need succumb passively to the exigencies of the next invention. Yet an invention which seems to make any aspect of living easier—and for "living" read making money, exercising power, as well as rearing children and seeking meaning—will be accepted and maintained until a better invention is made. It is quite useless to preach to a people whose fragile, poorly fired clay pots crack easily that they should not replace them with ugly factory-made but more permanent vessels or that thatch, which must be replaced every five years, is much more attractive than corrugated iron. People who have laboriously paddled their canoes up turbulent streams for five thousand years are going to welcome outboard motors even though there are no spare parts available and the motors will last only a few months. Zippers that can zip a fidgeting child into a snowsuit will replace buttons that have to be fastened one by one as surely as cars and telephones replaced horses and couriers.

True, some correctives have been developed. Computers have made it possible for planners to think much faster about more things than any single human mind could have before. It is now possible to do cost-benefit analyses which demonstrate that the Anglo-French SST Concorde plane is uneconomical, dangerous, and polluting, and that even when national prestige is weighed into the balance, the cost is too great. Each time the cars in a city like New York are temporarily banished from the streets by snow, the benefits in quiet and clean air are noted. The advantages of building a new lumber plant that does not pollute over maintaining an outdated one that does can be calculated. The use of these cost-benefit analyses, with human costs inexpertly counted in, has been growing, as the use of computers grows. They were little prophetic preparations for change, making the path of change straighter. But without the disappearance of cheap oil, the prospects were poor. The energy crisis has made it possible for the growing disillusionment with large-scale industrialization powered by fossil fuels to make itself felt.

As we turn to other sources of energy for the first time since the industrial revolution, technology will be on the side of decentralization and localization of productivity. There is undoubtedly some kind of technological limit—for example, to bigger and better windmills and solar collectors—a limit which the great automotive corporations of Detroit seem unable ever to set—even when thousands of defective cars have to be recalled. Perhaps the need to recall these thousands of cars—itself a product of greater awareness of the human price of too large a scale of manufacturing—will help reverse the trend also, but it is doubtful if any of the many small voices, crying in the wilderness, would have been heard in time were it not for the energy crisis.

But even so, the battle is anything but won. The voices of reason can speak for the use of some form of safe, renewable energy—solar, wind, diathermal. Those who would welcome the establishment of a world-wide way of life, in which things are made near the people who use them, crops grown by the people who eat them, and human beings live together in greater diversity, can rejoice over the possibilities opened by the energy crisis. But the same energy crisis opens the way also to the reckless proliferation of nuclear power.

There are many plausible arguments for presenting nuclear power as the solution to the energy crisis. It is less routinely polluting than the coal proposed as an interim solution. The massive disasters, so long predicted, have not happened yet. It can be argued that methods of dealing with deadly radioactive waste may be found. And there are huge profits involved for those who control it, in money or in political power, proportionate to the size and cost of the plants.

We have a chance today to turn back from the ruinous course we have followed since World War II, which fastened an earth-destroying, poverty-creating system on the world, but it is only a chance, and the existence of the nuclear alternative makes the outcome very much in doubt. It will take every effort of every person who knows and cares about the future of this planet, if we are to move toward the technological decentralization which may save it.

But in a world in which fear of the next generation and fear of overpopulation is rampant, where will that effort come from? We have to recapture the vision of a warless world which came with the first atomic bomb, carried through the unfortified skies to destroy Hiroshima. The vision of a warless world, then, was based on the sudden recognition that the skies were indeed indefensible. And it was that vision which inspired those who wrote President Dwight Eisenhower's "open skies" speech, delivered at the 1955 Big-Four Summit Meeting at Geneva. It was that vision which made the late Dr. Frank Fremont-Smith, a medical foundation executive, suggest as a basis for the early discussions with the Russians, the simple formula "Babies are okay," a shorthand version of the recognition that each of us, Russians and Americans, held the lives of the others in our hands, and that each must defend the children of the other or all would be destroyed. This is the humane version of deterrence, while the compounding of weapons for redestruction of the already destroyed is the inhumane. But for a brief period we did glimpse a world where war would indeed have been unthinkable. Then we forgot again and concentrated on bases and targeted multiple warheads.

It will be necessary to concentrate again on the earth's atmosphere and the extent to which all that is most dangerous and all that binds one people to another goes through the air. If we keep our minds firmly on the nature of the thin cover that protects life on earth, we can then go back and look at the history of human warfare, the development of empires, and the values for which human beings have been willing to sacrifice life itself.

Among the very simplest peoples that we know, there is some recognition of territory and of privacy, of space that must not be violated. It may be very slight, simply the ground on which a tired woman sits down after a day of walking through the jungle and gathers her children around her for an evening meal. Or it may be a sapling shaped into an arch to make a doorway where there are no walls, simply a hollow in the desert sand where a group of Kalihari Bushmen have settled in for the night. But the attachment to some home place is there, and it is extended also to some feeling for one's own territory, one's own hunting and gathering grounds. As civilization developed and people became more sedentary, this sense of one's own country became more defined, and in time frontiers which men were willing to defend were demarcated. The defense of frontiers became not only the defense of home and gardens and of hunting, gathering, and fishing grounds, and of the women and children, but in later times the same willingness to defend to the death the traditions of a people, their language, their religion, their whole way of life. Throughout the ages, the call to defend these shared and precious things have found men ready to lay down their lives and women willing to send their sons and husbands out to die—for the future.

Throughout history, rapacious groups have reached out for the territory of other weaker groups, with defense calling forth a deeper commitment than attack and attacks which violated the contemporary standards of human ethics calling forth a deeper loss of ethics and destructiveness. So aggressive war is accompanied by rape and arson, as the enemy's men were put to the sword or carried off to slavery, women raped and captured, cities burned to the ground and the good earth scorched. The accompaniment of defensive warfare—and by this I mean warfare that is seen as defensive, not warfare that is realistically defensive—has been great bravery and sacrifice, last stands—the Battle of Britain, the siege of Leningrad—and peoples willing to retreat to infertile and hostile habitats to live as they believe they should live. The accompaniments of aggressive warfare have been massacres—Nanking, Lidice, My Lai. But the ease with which aggression can be rationalized as defense and the confusion that surrounds such rationalization have meant a tremendous lack of clarity about human beings' capabilities for good or evil. Instead of looking at the contexts within which human beings act and at their capacities for protective, sacrificial, rapacious, destructive, or merely self-centered behavior, biologists keep advising us that we should look at the nature of man and how genetically determined altruistic or selfish behavior has developed and been regulated. Each set of claims on the subject engenders a violent argument, as those who claim that human beings are naturally evil, to be constrained or genetically engineered, confront those who believe they are naturally good, but twisted and distorted by evil institutions.

But if we look at human history carefully, we find the same individual or a group of the same genetic composition behaving protectively and nobly at one time and destructively at another. If we look closely at the conditions of dedication and what heroic self-sacrifice human beings are capable of, then the question we have to ask is "Can we create, on a world scale, the conditions which make our historic capacities for defending and maintaining our own group available for the whole planet?" The great religions are great simply because they have transcended narrow loyalties of race and language, homeland, and tradition, as they have spread from one people to another. But head-on collisions between the great religions, each emphasizing the brotherhood of all human beings, have in the end resulted in bloodshed, often among themselves as well. Groups, each proclaiming the brotherhood of man, have prayed for the death of their "brethren" and blessed the weapons that would destroy

them, from Christian prayers on both sides of medieval battles, to the American A-bombing of Nagasaki at the end of
World War II. Within Buddhism and Islam, as well as within
Christianity, the proclaimed "brotherhood" has not been
sufficient. How then are the loyalties to home and community
and country ever to be extended to include the endangered
human race? To do this, we need both economic and technological conditions and a new vision. With our inveterate
desire to dichotomize and polarize, contemporary prophets
keep advocating one or the other, when in fact, we need
both.

As long as human beings depended upon safety on the
ground and the sea, defense of frontiers seemed inevitable.
Two houses could not be built on the same ground, or two
trees planted in the same spot, or two piers extended from
the same narrow bit of shore into the sea, or two ships take
refuge in a harbor large enough for only one. Although we
have succeeded in uniting millions in nation states within
which each citizen could identify with all the others though
never seen and often very different but united in citizenship,
how were we to deal, either conceptually or realistically,
with competition for resources on land and water in a heavily
populated world? And if we couldn't deal with them but continued to live in a world in which major wars might be contained, would we have to have a rash of "minor" wars to
starve or kill millions and devastate cities and forests and
pasture land? The virtues of defensive war were inextricably
mixed, and often provocative of, the rapaciousness of offen-
sive wars. Were we committed to a world in which the super
powers armed both sides of a conflict in the pursuit of
"peace"?

This dilemma, the evils of misplaced patriotism, and the
opposition which the patriot feels toward any sort of interna-
tionalism which would denigrate or deny his patriotism, has
informed the discussions about world order, ever since it became apparent that some sort of planetary order would be

necessary if life was to be preserved in an intercommunicating planetary community.

Today, the two outstanding technical changes—first, in sources of energy and the need for environmental protection that make localization economically necessary and, secondly, in the shift of warfare and communication from land and sea to the air—make it possible to resolve this war-peace dilemma. The shift in scale, from huge impersonal factories exporting their products halfway round the world to the need to localize production near the point of use, will make it possible to reinforce the intimate interdependency of human beings who again live in community, working and living close together, capable of developing the kind of ties which can be extended from household to community to country. The overwhelming importance of the atmosphere means that there are no longer any frontiers to defend against pollution, attack, or propaganda. It means, further, that only by a deep patriotic devotion to one's own country can there be a hope of the kind of protection of the whole planet, which is necessary for the survival of the people of other countries. If we care enough about our children to see that the air they breathe is pure and about our own soil to see that it is not washed away into the sea, enough about our own lakes and rivers and coastal waters to protect them from pollution and death, we will in turn be protecting the children of our neighbors. So both patriotic devotion and concern for the planet shift our defenses to inside the country, away from those once so jealously guarded frontiers. Only if every country refrains from sending up into the atmosphere substances that may destroy our ozone layer, only if every country refrains from mischievous weather modification, only if all countries forbid release of radioactivity into the air can the planet be protected. So, perhaps for the first time in human history, since a few male creatures defended their females and offspring from predators, human beings' instincts need no longer be enlisted in causes which result in the destruction of others.

The new technologies can begin to provide a framework to answer the anguished cry of that fifteen-year-old boy of the 1960s, member of the first wave of the new generation, who insisted: "There must be a better way and we have to find it."

CHAPTER NINE

Safeguarding Diversity

There are far deeper problems than those that involve com-
bating the immediate dangers of nuclear war, nuclear proliferation, permanent irreversible environmental damage, and
deterioration of the quality of life. These hazards are very
grave. The need to prevent the destruction of civilization, if
not life itself, is urgent and overriding. Although survival is
the absolute necessity for the further development of the
human experience, too much concentration on survival, besides actively making that survival less likely, can in a subtle
way blur our vision, because somehow we have demeaned
ourselves in the process. To the statement, "Man does not
live by bread alone," must be added "Man does not live by
life alone"—something the great religions have always
preached, each in its limited, time-bound way.

There are new technological conditions within which a
new initiative for the human race is possible. But it will not
be found without a new vision. The historic figures of speech
of "brotherhood" and "sisterhood," of loyalty to kin, which
the great religions have used, are no longer enough. As my
daughter Catherine Bateson has pointed out, the image of a
group of brothers and sisters, although it has carried the
great religions forward for several thousand years, is in fact
too narrow and leaves out a group to which human beings
have been equally bound throughout human evolution—
those others whom they marry and brothers-in-law and
sisters-in-law.

To the age-old vision of one's own home fires, one's own
kin, one's own community, and one's own country, to be

loved, defended, and sustained against all odds, we can now add a vision of a planetary community all living within one atmosphere, encircled by air currents that carry danger in one part of the world to another part, all of which must be protected if any are to be protected. And for the great religious vision which has been partially embodied in the idea of human brotherhood, we have now the vision of human community, male and female, kin and nonkin, who together make up the unity of the human race. Within such a vision, the contributions of each culture, of the search for spirituality and grace in some parts of the world and the search for good works and the earthly well-being of human beings in other parts of the world, can become complementary.

Such a vision and the search for music to hail it, figures of speech to interpret it, styles of life to embody it, should be enough to evoke the strongest commitment the world has ever seen. Our vision has enlarged as our political communities have enlarged; our capacity to call men "brothers" or "fellow citizens," no matter what their physique or whether we would recognize them if we met, has grown. Cultural evolution has seen an enormous enlargement of the human spirit, an enlargement which has been intimately related to the number and diversity of those whom we could include within our expanding frontiers of shared dedication.

However, such expansion has been matched, throughout human history, by an expansion in the numbers of those who were outside—the infidel, the enemy. But within the new vision, there must be no outsiders. Postfiguration, cofiguration, and prefiguration are all partial ways in which fragmented, diverse, human societies scattered over the surface of the earth have transmitted and elaborated their cultural traditions. During the long course of our history we have been able to survive and to deplete the earth, though it was not fatally injured. But now we have become one intercommunicating whole, equipped with lethal powers to destroy life itself. Prefiguration itself is new and we have hardly begun to know how to include the young within the decisions of their elders. But already more portentous decisions are upon us.

Unless we can develop a new vision in which each one of us and each segment of humanity, whether it be a nation state, an age group, or a religious or ideological group, can become complementary and not competitive with each other, we run the new risk of destroying life as we reach for artificial ways of enhancing it—by playing God, by manufacturing plutonium against which earth holds no protective antidote, by manufacturing nonbiodegradable chemicals, and by planning to manipulate the very stuff of our long biological inheritance into unknown and possibly lethal forms. The uses of power, the search for power, the definition of power, all are as old as human history. But we are overused to the familiar statement, "Power tends to corrupt and absolute power corrupts absolutely." We can also add, "Responsibility tends to ennoble and absolute responsibility ennobles absolutely." With the new powers conferred upon mankind by the natural sciences—and I use the term *man*kind here advisedly, for women have played a very slight role in developing the sciences so far—we are faced squarely with the decision of whether to reach for naked power heedless of the consequences or whether to exercise these powers as custodians of the future.

In human beings' long struggle to relate to the universe, their appeals to transcendent powers have taken many forms. They have assumed an inherent order in the universe within which human beings could live safely if only that order was respected; they have petitioned and sacrificed to deities whose favor and blessing they sought and whose wrath they have attempted to avert; they have developed magical formulas believed potent enough to coerce the natural world, to seduce the unwilling wives of other men, to make plants grow or wither away, to make the rain fall or the sun shine. Magic has sometimes been regarded as the precursor of science, and to the extent that scientists have behaved like magicians, such science has been inimicable to the well-being of human kind. When science becomes magic, all powerful, subject to neither reverence for life nor respect for the natural world, such science is man playing God as surely as the garden magician muttering charms into a leaf to lure his neighbor's yams into his garden or to force his neighbor's wife to leave her husband is playing God.

Difference between these three religious attitudes lay entirely in the attitudes of the practitioners—human beings as seekers of divine support, human beings as respectors of a cosmic order, or human beings as petty rulers in possession of the secrets of power. Often the three attitudes occurred within the same culture; the same practitioner might at one time invoke one, then another, approach to the attainment of his hopes and desires, although there was a tendency for the practice of magic to be private and secret, the pursuit of personal rather than social ends.

Likewise, within science there are those scientists who work with reverence and respect for the natural world, not seeing themselves as omnipotent invaders or intruders, but there are also those who wish to replace the cosmic order, as it is expressed in the delicate balances of the biosphere, by man-made manipulations in which they in effect become gods, deciding on the fate of the whole human phenomenon. Herein the danger lies, and one may ask what recourse do human beings have against politicians without commitment beyond their terms of office, aided and abetted by some of the scientists who now have the knowledge to destroy the world.

All over the world people are struggling with parts of this problem, and a major task is to state it as a whole, so that each fragmented approach can fit into place. Stated at its simplest, any whole system—a single organism, an island ecosystem, our planet, the solar system—is subject to imbalances within itself. For millennia, human beings on earth lived in small scattered groups, each one struggling to survive, each one failing or succeeding as it remained in or out of balance with its neighbors and the natural world. Drought and flood threatened the groups' food supply; earthquakes, hurricanes, and volcanic eruptions threatened their lives. Those who survived were able to adjust to changed conditions, to control their population growth, to shift their food dependence, to learn from new neighbors.

Although we do not have full records of these early communities, we know a good deal about the hunting-and-gathering peoples who lived under the same kind of technological constraints and with comparable cultural, political, and social forms. In such societies there are provisions for the weak and the ill, provisions for reconciliation between personalities, provisions for contraction or expansion as circumstances dictate. The societies' survival, like the survival of any species depends upon their response to both favorable and unfavorable conditions. Men and women, young and old, contributed in culturally patterned ways to the survival of the whole.

As civilizations developed, this balance between all the members of a group and the ecosystem of which they were a part was disturbed. Whole populations were enslaved. Whole regions were desolated by demands made on the forests and the soil. As people were concentrated in greater densities, they became more liable to plague and more subject to internal political disorders as one faction fought with another to attain or retain power. Slowly, immense changes were made in the human relationship to the ecosystem of the earth; fire was used as a way of hunting and clearing for gardens; minerals were mined; soil eroded after deforestation and harbors were silted up; animals and plants were domesticated and bred, with new species developed that were more specialized, more fragile than their wild predecessors.

Throughout these millennia when we were learning to be more human, in the sense that knowledge and skill are ennobling human characteristics, countless small human groups disappeared and the foods they had depended upon and the animals they hunted sometimes became, like themselves, extinct. But the whole evolutionary process went on, no part able by its failure to endanger the whole. For thousands of years in the Americas, a parallel development of astronomy, record keeping, architecture, agriculture, and the skills in governing large populations developed independent of the same kind of cultural evolution in the Old World. Either could have been wiped out without endangering the other, and within the Old World and the New World empires rose and fell also.

Today, however, we face an entirely new and unprecedented situation. The same series of events that made it possible to invent nuclear power and to explore the entire world, establish world-wide communication, and explore outer space resulted in the Generation Gap, as young and old were separated by the extraordinary differences in their experiences. Instead of congeries of small groups of people punctuated by periods of urbanization and subsequent decline, as the magnificent cities of the Cretans or the Mayans disintegrated and the descendants of those who had built them became simple peasants again, ignorant of scripts used by their predecessors, there are now interconnected, interdependent world communities, which respond as all interconnected systems do —as a whole, to a disturbance *at any point.* The hijacking of a single plane any place is reflected on every continent and a total strike of the world's airline pilots would cost billions and wreak havoc in the largest cities and the smallest villages, as vaccines failed to arrive and epidemics were unloosed, contracts fell through, revolutions failed and other revolutions succeeded, men on whose lives millions depended died as one surgeon failed to arrive.

Within this newly interconnected planetary system we have the task of making it less vulnerable to disruption, either by sudden events or because we have by our own interventions made it more homogeneous and therefore more vulnerable. The period since World War II has been characterized by an enormous spread of uniformities, of monocrops where hundreds of acres are sown with the same artificially engineered seed and dependent upon huge amounts of fertilizer and pesticides, and food animals bred for the slaughter house, of giant electric-power grids in which a single failure may affect millions of people.

Yet if we turn to the findings of biologists on the ecology of the planet, we find diversity as an essential ingredient of survival. Any reduction in diversity represents a hazard. Experimentalists interested in genetic engineering now speak of the need to *manufacture* diversity; ecologists seek to preserve, in seed banks and zoos, the great variety of genes from the wild forms which are disappearing. Anthropologists make the same kind of plea for the use of tape, film, and video to preserve forms of music and art, speech and posture, which human beings developed through thousands of years and today are stored only in the minds and muscles of those who have learned them. Once the life style changes, all these traditional forms will be gone forever, and those who should have inherited them and all the world will be the poorer.

But we need something far greater than diversity; we need a transcendent value that can contain our obstreperous and promiscuous experimentation, guide it without stifling it, that can keep free man's willingness to climb the highest mountain and take the first feasible vessel to the moon, probe the smallest cell as well as the greatest distances in space. The demand that such explorations be forbidden cuts at the very root of those qualities in human beings to which we owe the civilizations that make us proud. We do not need ways to keep scientists and explorers down, but ways in which they can be ennobled in their very pursuits by sharing in a common responsibility, a responsibility which must not be placed on scientists alone but which must be shared by every citizen of Earth.

Fascinatingly enough, because systems are in fact systematic, the very burgeoning of science that has resulted in world-wide diffusion of a monotonous modern culture has also stimulated people throughout the world to demand participation. And through this demand for participation in the benefits of a monotonous, homogeneous technology, we have

actually generated new ways to preserve diversity. Where
the controls have become overspecialized in the hands of the
politicians, scientists, and clergy of one culture or in one
religion or ideology, in one class, one sex or one age group,
the safety of the whole has been grievously endangered.
Where older men send the flower of youth into battle, make
laws forbidding women the use of contraceptives, scientists
tinker with the safety of an entire community to win a Nobel
prize by manipulating *Escherichia coli,* young men force
older men into a retirement that kills, employers exploit em-
ployees or minorities blackmail timid officials. In fact, where
any one group, excluding others, takes control for its own
interests, the body politic is as surely endangered as is the
human body when a cancer begins to grow. A viable balance
demands the participation of *all* of those who form part of a
system, not only of those who have temporarily got control of
a part of it. Neither can we build a viable polity by trade-offs
among interest groups, sometimes called "the decisions of the
market place"—trade-offs among those seeking privilege,
power, and national prestige.

This new phase of human history, which began in the mid-
1940s, resulted in the division of the young from the old and
the females from the males and in the political recognition of
even the smallest and most remote human groups, and the
first voices of these new groups sound raucous and irresponsible and as competitive as the old imperialisms of age
or sex or race and nationality against which they are
rebelling. Whether it be the Eskimo demanding the right to
kill whales with new weapons that will very soon destroy all
the whales on which they depend for food, or the elite of a
developing country happily welcoming a polluting industry,
or quick-buck entrepreneurs claiming pornography to be free-
dom of speech, superficially it is not a pretty scene.

But beyond and beneath the contemporary first stages of
participation with their emphases on grievance and restitu-
tion and a share of a material pie, beyond the greediness of
the recently hungry and the fury of those who have just dis-

covered the full measure of previous oppression, a new ethic is growing up. In this new ethic, the people of each part of the world, north and south, east and west, are being asked to accept responsibility for each other.

It is not only participation in the material gains and freedoms which are being demanded by the world's people but also the dignity of sharing in all decisions that affect a person's own life and that of his or her kin and neighbors, descendants and successors. And with the demand for participation will come, inevitably, contributions from each to the whole. Women, in demanding recognition at every political level, can again contribute, as they still do in small subsistence communities, to decisions about food, which today, left in the hands of men, lack the element of conservation and care for individual human beings for which women have been traditionally responsible. Participation for every group —male and female, young, middle-aged, and old, African, Asian, and Caucasian—means a meeting between producer and consumer, ruler and ruled, victim and erstwhile oppressor, those pushed out of office and those who succeed them. By the simple demand that they be there, they be consulted, they be recognized, and they be treated with dignity, all the diverse groups hitherto excluded from the council tables of the civilized, stratified, multileveled world will make some contribution to the decisions that are made. If each group is accepted for its uniqueness, then they all will inevitably complement each other. We will be able to achieve the diversity and therefore the wholeness of collective human behavior, in which each age, both sexes, and the representatives of those different cultures, each with hundreds of years of history behind it, have a place. The search for uniformity, for styles of behavior for young and old, learned and preliterate, for students who are ranked on a single intelligence test, as inevitably produces competitiveness on single scales of acquisition or achievement as competitiveness itself is standardizing. So the participation of groups that are inherently diverse will bring different visions and different experience to the decision-making centers of the world.

So with each demand for social justice, for human rights, for atonement of past wrongs, for righting previous wrongs, for heeding the freshness of the young or the wisdom of the old, there comes an implicit promise. It is seldom indeed that these promises are made explicit in these first stages of building safety for our endangered interconnected world—but each promise helps to create balance within the new whole to which we all belong. These contributions can become as systemic as previous failures to take the whole into account where multinational operating corporations or armed nation-states pursued their narrow interests at the expense of the whole. The planetary community is now made up of *all* the inhabitants of the planet, its wholeness and safety dependent upon all of them. One group, one nation, even one individual who acts in defiance of the needs of the whole, can endanger the whole. It is as if the earth were a sphere made up of strangely shaped mosaic pieces which, by fitting together, hold it together and where the withdrawal of one piece might result in the sphere's collapse. The knowledge that this is so can provide us with the energy to keep each part in place, but only if that knowledge is shared by all the others. Even the contemporary demand for the right of participation for the handicapped makes its contribution to mutual understanding, as those who are blind bring an extra acuteness of hearing and those who are deaf bring an extra visual perceptiveness. With every inclusion of the hitherto excluded— whether it be a paraplegic, a woman, an old man of ninety, a Pygmy from the Ituri forest, a shaman from the Amazonian jungle, or a dancer from the Nubian desert—the human community, grown richer, more intricately related and diverse, will have a better chance of survival and growth.

If we know how to cherish and cultivate this urge for participation until it becomes a safeguard of human evolution, then we can contain the kind of exploitative engineering and power-seeking, profit-seeking, prestige-seeking motives which produce runaway feedbacks that threaten the whole planet. It will become impossible to sacrifice one group for another, for everyone will be there. One of the great discoveries of anthropology during World War II was that we always had to speak and write as if everyone were listening. Today the demand that everyone listen and be listened to is the hope of an endangered but potentially self-healing world.

APPENDIX A

Bibliographical Note

Part I, the original version of this book, published under the title of *Culture and Commitment: A Study of the Generation Gap,* was based on my lectures in the *Man and Nature* series at The American Museum of Natural History in March 1969 in conjunction with the Museum's centennial celebration. Conceived of as a lecture series with a week's gap in between, a different type of transition was needed for a book designed to be read at one sitting. The third lecture was published in *Science, 164* (No. 3876, April 1969, p. 135) under the title "The Generation Gap." This separate essay style has been preserved in Part II of the new edition. The Doubleday paperback edition, in which the subtitle was dropped at the initiative of the publisher, was published in 1970. Foreign editions, interesting for their interpretations of the title have been published as:

> *Cultura y Compromiso.* Buenos Aires: Granica, 1970 (Argentinian edition).
> *Kultur og Engagement.* Copenhagen: Schultz, 1970 (Danish edition).
> *Ikäryhmien ristiriidat.* Helsinki: Kustannusosakeyhtiö Otava, 1971 (Finnish edition).
> *Le Fosse des Générations.* Paris: Denöel, 1971 (French edition).
> *Der Konflikt der Generationen.* Munich and Stuttgart: Klett, 1970; Munich: Deutscher Taschenbuch Verlag, 1974 (German editions).
> *Generazioni in Conflitto.* Milan: Rizzoli, 1972 (Italian edition).

Broen over Generasjons Kløffen. Oslo: Universitetsforlaget, 1971 (Norwegian edition).

Kultur och engagemang. Stockholm: Rabén and Sjögren, 1970 (Swedish edition).

Der Konflikt der Generationen. Olten: Walter, 1971 (Swiss edition).

I have only revised Part I to remove confusing anachronisms. Otherwise, I have left it as a statement of the general argument and the future as it appeared in the late 1960s.

I have published extensive bibliographies on my own field work and the publications of others on the same peoples in "Social Organization of Manua," *Bernice P. Bishop Museum Bulletin, 76* (Honolulu, 1930); in *Male and Female* (New York: Morrow, 1949; New York: Dell, 1968); and in *Continuities in Cultural Evolution* (New Haven: Yale University Press, 1964). *Margaret Mead: The Complete Bibliography 1925–1975,* edited by Joan Gordan (The Hague: Mouton, 1976) contains a complete listing of my writings.

I have made partial acknowledgment of my intellectual indebtedness in the preface and the references cited in *Continuities in Cultural Evolution.* In *An Anthropologist at Work: Writings of Ruth Benedict* (Boston: Houghton Mifflin, 1959; New York: Atherton, 1966) I have given a more detailed account of the early period at Columbia University when our first understanding was being formed of how culture is transmitted. My chapter, "Margaret Mead," in *A History of Psychology in Autobiography,* Volume VI, edited by Gardner Lindzey (New York: Prentice-Hall, 1974, pp. 293–326), discusses my specific debt to psychologists.

The selected set of essays *Anthropology: A Human Science* (Princeton: Van Nostrand, 1964) details in part the development of my understanding of cultural character and some of the measures I have thought must be taken in applying our growing understanding of culture to man's present precarious situation.

My understanding of the differential roles in the acculturative process played by grandparents, parents, and children developed slowly. I first discussed confusions of cofigurative cultures in "Education for Choice," Chapter 14, in *Coming of Age in Samoa* (New York: Morrow, 1928; New York: Dell, 1968). Shifts in sanctions and surrogates are discussed in "Social Change and Cultural Surrogates," *Journal of Educational Sociology, 14* (1940, pp. 92–109); "Age Patterning in Personality Development," *American Journal of Orthopsychiatry, 17* (1947, pp. 231–40); "The Implications of Culture Change for Personality Development," *American Journal of Orthopsychiatry, 17* (1947, pp. 633–46); "On the Implications for Anthropology of the Gesell-Ilg Approach to Maturation," *American Anthropologist, 49* (1947, pp. 69–77); "Character Formation and Diachronic Theory," in *Social Structure: Studies Presented to A. R. Radcliffe-Brown,* edited by Meyer Fortes (Oxford: Clarendon Press, 1949); "The Impact of Culture on Personality Development in the United States Today," in *Midcentury White House Conference on Children and Youth, Proceedings of the Report of Conference Sessions, Washington, D.C., December 3–7, 1950,* edited by E. A. Richards (Raleigh, N.C.: Health Publications Institute, 1951, pp. 84–86); and in *The School in American Culture* (Cambridge, Mass.: Harvard University Press, 1951; reissued 1964). *And Keep Your Powder Dry* (New York: Morrow, 1942; paperback, 1965) spelled out relations of immigration to character formation in the United States.

I first used the terms *prefigurative, cofigurative,* and *postfigurative* in "Cultural Determinants of Sexual Behavior," in *Sex and Internal Secretions,* edited by W. C. Young (2 vols., 3d ed., Baltimore: Williams and Wilkins, 1961, vol. 2, pp. 1433–79). In "Towards More Vivid Utopias," *Science, 126* (November 8, 1957, pp. 957–61); "Closing the Gap Between the Scientists and the Others," *Daedalus* (Winter 1959, pp. 139–46); and "The Future as the Basis for Establishing a Shared Culture," *Daedalus* (Winter 1965, pp. 135–55), I began to develop the idea of the way the learning of children reinforms adults' understanding of their culture. *New Lives for Old: Cultural Transformation—Manus, 1928–1953* (New York: Morrow, 1956; New York, Dell, 1968) describes how one New Guinea people moved from the stone age into the present.

Some of the ideas which I have developed in Part II have been discussed in more detail in "The Kalinga Prize," *Journal of World History, 13* (1971, pp. 765–71); "Revolution–Evolution: Impact on the Family," Acceptance Speech, Wilder Penfield Award (Toronto, Canada: Vanier Institute, 1972, mimeographed); with Ken Heyman, *World Enough: Rethinking the Future* (Boston: Little, Brown, 1975); "Return to Manus," *Natural History, 85* (June–July 1976, pp. 60–69); "Towards a Human Science," *Science, 191* (March 5, 1976, pp. 903–9); "Prospects for World Harmony," *Indian and Foreign Review, 11* (December 1973, pp. 20–21); and as editor, with William W. Kellogg, *The Atmosphere: Endangered and Endangering,* Fogarty International Center Proceedings No. 39 (Washington, D.C.: U. S. Government Printing Office, ✗017-053-0059-1, 1977).

My first understanding of what was to come was expressed, I believe, in a poem I wrote in the 1920s, *And Your Young Men Shall See Visions:*

"We have no past for fuel." The young men said.
"We have no long and dry array of husk-like hours,
  To bind in faggots, furbished for a pyre
  Where all our dead days blossom into flowers
  Of dream, renascent in the mighty fire."

"Cut then your future down!" The old men said.
"Fell the tall loveliness of unlived days;
  In such a smoke, new fathered of the green,
  Unsullied wood, in secret perilous ways,
  The unremembering young have visions seen."

My first formulation of the parental role, written in 1947, was my last poem:

For Mary Catherine Bateson

That I be not a restless ghost
Who haunts your footsteps as they pass
Beyond the point where you have left
Me standing in the newsprung grass,

You must be free to take a path
Whose end I feel no need to know,
No irking fever to be sure
You went where I would have you go.

Those who would fence the future in
Between two walls of well-laid stones
But lay a ghost walk for themselves,
A dreary walk for dusty bones.

So you can go without regret
Away from this familiar land,
Leaving your kiss upon my hair
And all the future in your hands.

Films, Slides, and Music
Used in the *Man and Nature* Lectures

When I gave the *Man and Nature* lectures in March 1969, I used short sequences from films, slides, and a music tape to supplement my own words. They are part of the record of what I wished to convey, but cannot be included, except as references, in the published version.

LECTURE I *The Past—Postfigurative Cultures and Well-Known Forebears*

BALIKCI, ASEN, and QUENTIN BROWN. Parts from *Fishing at the Stone Weir,* The Netsilik Eskimo Film Series, Educational Services Inc., 16mm., Parts I and II, color, 1966.

MEAD, MARGARET, and GREGORY BATESON. Iatmul sequence National Film Board of Canada, distributed by McGraw-Hill, 16mm., black and white, sound, 1959.

MEAD, MARGARET, and GREGORY BATESON. Iatmul sequence from *Bathing Babies in Three Cultures,* Character Formation in Different Cultures Series, New York University Film Library, 16mm., black and white, sound, 1952.

LECTURE II *The Present—Cofigurative Cultures and Familiar Peers*

LOMAX, ALAN. Tapes specially prepared from the findings of Canometrics; excerpts demonstrating solo songs from Manus and Ibiza and black spirituals from the United States; Lomax recordings, not for distribution.

MEAD, MARGARET collection. Slides on Manus, hand-painted in color, 1928, 1953, 1967.

Oss, Oss, Wee Oss. Country Dance Society of America, 16mm., color, sound, 1950.

LECTURE III *The Future—Prefigurative Cultures and Unknown Children*

BATESON, GREGORY. *Security,* unpublished film of children's first experience with death, 16mm., black and white, 1941.

CLAH, AL. *Intrepid Shadows,* Sol Worth and John Adair, producers, Philadelphia: Annenberg School of Communication, University of Pennsylvania; part of series of seven films "Navajo Film Themselves," 16 mm., black and white, 1966.

Not Much to Do. Privately made; a film planned and excuted by four black teen-agers; 16 mm., black and white, sound, 1966.

Related Readings

ABEL, THEODORA M., and RHODA METRAUX. *Culture and Psychotherapy*. New Haven: Yale College and University Press, 1974.

American Association for the Advancement of Science. *The Cultural Consequences of Population Change*. Washington, D.C.: The Center for the Study of Man, Smithsonian Institution, 1975. Pamphlet.

———. *Culture and Population Change*. Washington, D.C.: American Association for the Advancement of Science, 1974. Pamphlet.

BATESON, GREGORY. *Steps to an Ecology of Mind*. San Francisco: Chandler, 1972.

BATESON, MARY CATHERINE. *Our Own Metaphor*. New York: Knopf, 1972.

BROCKMAN, JOHN, ed. *About Bateson*. New York: Dutton, 1977.

BROWN, LESTER. *By Bread Alone*. Elmsford, N.Y.: Pergamon, 1976.

CARSON, RACHEL. *Silent Spring*. Boston: Houghton Mifflin, 1962.

CHICHILNISKY, G., J. E. HARDOY, and A. O. HERRERA. *Catastrophe or New Society? A Latin American World Model*. Ottawa, Can.: International Development Research Center, 1976.

COBB, EDITH. *The Ecology of Imagination in Childhood*. New York: Columbia University Press, 1977.

COMMONER, BARRY. *The Closing Circle*. New York: Knopf, 1971.

———. *The Poverty of Power*. New York: Knopf, 1976.

DUBOS, RENÉ. *Of Human Diversity*. Heinz Werner Lecture Series, vol. 3. Barre, Mass.: Barre, 1974.

EISELEY, LOREN C. *The Immense Journey*. New York: Random House, 1957.

ERIKSON, ERIK. *Childhood and Society*. Rev. ed. New York: Norton, 1963.

———. *Identity: Youth and Crisis*. New York: Norton, 1968.

———. *Toys and Reasons*. New York: Norton, 1977.

GOODFIELD, JUNE. *Playing God: Genetic Engineering and the Manipulation of Life*. New York: Random House, 1977.

GORER, GEOFFREY. *Death, Grief and Mourning*. Garden City, N.Y.: Doubleday, 1965; Anchor paperback, 1967.

HAUGHEY, JOHN C. *Should Anyone Say Forever: Making, Keeping, Breaking Commitments*. Garden City, N.Y.: Doubleday, 1975.

HUXLEY, THOMAS H., and JULIAN S. HUXLEY. *Touchstone for Ethics*. New York: Harper, 1947.

KENNISTON, KENNETH. *Youth and Dissent: The Rise of a New Opposition*. New York: Harcourt, Brace, Jovanovich, 1971.

LAND, GEORGE T. *Grow or Die*. New York: Random House, 1973.

LASZLO, ERVIN, et al., eds. *Goals for Mankind: A Report to the Club of Rome on the New Horizons of Global Community*. New York: Dutton, 1977.

LOVINS, AMORY B. *Soft Energy Paths*. Cambridge, Mass. Friends of the Earth Ballinger Publishing, 1977.

MEADOWS, DONELLA H., et al. *Limits to Growth: Report of the Club of Rome's Project on the Predicament of Mankind*. New York: Universe Books, 1972.

MESAROVIC, MIHAJLO, and E. C. PESTEL. *Mankind at the Turning Point*. New York: Readers Digest Press, 1974.

MOSELY, PHILIP E. *The Kremlin and World Politics: Studies in Soviet Policy and Action*. New York: Vintage, 1960.

OLTMANS, WILLEM, ed. *On Growth*. New York: Putnam, 1974.

POGGIE, JOHN J., and ROBERT N. LYNCH, eds. *Rethinking Modernization: Anthropological Perspectives.* Westport and London: Greenwood, 1974.

ROE, ANNE, and GEORGE GAYLORD SIMPSON. *Behavior and Evolution.* New Haven: Yale University Press, 1958.

ROTHCHILD, JOHN, and SUSAN BERNS WOLF. *The Children of the Counterculture.* Garden City, N.Y.: Doubleday, 1976.

THOMAS, LEWIS. *Lives of a Cell.* New York: Viking, 1974.

WADDINGTON, C. H., ed. *Biology and the History of the Future.* Edinburgh: Edinburgh University Press, 1972.

———. *The Ethical Animal.* Chicago: University of Chicago Press, 1961.

———. *Tools for Thought.* New York: Harper & Row, 1977.

WARD, BARBARA, and RENÉ DUBOS. *Only One Earth: The Care and Maintenance of a Small Planet.* New York: Norton, 1972.

WOLFENSTEIN, MARTHA, and NATHAN LEITES. *The Movies: A Psychological Study.* Glencoe, Ill.: Free Press, 1950.

Index

Index

Abkasian people, 123
Aborigines, Australian, 24–25,
    28, 54
Abortion, 111
Absolutism, 79, 80
Acid rock music, 117–18
Admiralty Islands, 50
Adolescent rebellion, 65–66
Afro hair-dos, 111
Airplane hijackings, 152
Algerian independence
    movement, 119
Alienation, 47, 77, 102, 109,
    115, 119, 122, 127, 128
Amish, 22–23
Anglo-French SST Concorde
    plane, 138
Apollo mission, 3
Appalachian people, 33–34
Arapesh people, 18–20, 22
Armenians, 16, 25, 29, 61
Arms exports industry, 100
Asavi, Kami, 52
Assumption of the Virgin Mary,
    doctrine of, 99
Atomic bomb, dropping of,
    71–72, 97, 100

Bali, 21–22, 25–26, 90
Banaro people, 28
Bateson, Catherine, 147
Bateson, Gregory, 136
Bathonga people, 26–27
Beards, 95

Betara Desa (god), 21
Bible, 135
Blackberry Winter (Mead),
    103
Blacks, 110
Black separatists, 81
Bronowski, Jacob, xvi
Buddhism, 21, 80, 143
Burglary, fear of, 111

California Indians, 24, 30
Cambodia, U.S. intervention in,
    97
Camus, Albert, 81
Capitalism, 65
Capital punishment, 112
Cash, Johnny, 117
Caste system (India), 16, 45
Catastrophes, 7–8, 14,
    150–51
Centralization, process of,
    136–37
Changelessness, change within,
    61–62
Childhood's End (Clarke), 88
Child nurses, 56
Children, pornographic
    exploitation of, 112
Children of the Counterculture,
    The (Rothchild and
    Wolf), 128
China, 66, 67, 77, 88–89, 104
Christianity, 143
Churchill, Winston, 130

Civil rights movement of
  1950s–1960s, 110, 119
Clarke, Arthur, 88
Clothing styles, 105, 106,
  115
Club of Rome, 119
Cofigurative cultures, 39–64,
  125
  absence of grandparents, 48,
    49
  alienating experiences, 47
  beginning of, 39–40
  breakdown of sanctions, 55
  change within changelessness,
    61–62
  children and, 40–41, 43, 49,
    56–57, 60, 64
  clothing styles, 42
  conditions for change, 40
  conflict between generations,
    43–47
  crossing of sex lines, 45–46
  cultural absorption, 40–41
  education and, 46–47, 57, 59
  elders and, 39, 40, 41, 43,
    48–49
  emergence of, 62
  idea of continuity, 42, 55–56
  keeping up with relationships,
    48–49
  links to the past, 49, 51
  maturation of growing child,
    57–59
  meaning of, 13, 39, 48
  migration and immigration,
    39–42, 59, 62, 63
  nuclear family and, 53–54,
    60–61
  nurturing relationships, 56–57
  rapid change and, 55, 59, 64
  retirement and removal of
    the elderly, 49
  stability, 42, 54
  in the United States, 59–61
  young generation compared

    to old, 42–43
College deans' offices, student
    demonstrations in, 106
Commitment, new forms of,
    121–32
Communes, 128, 129
Communist party (China), 66
Computer industry, 138
Computer science, 69
Conscientious objectors, 76
Conservatism, 125
  in child rearing, 56
Contraceptives, 154
Cost-benefit analyses, 138–39
Counterculture, 95
Cousins, Norman, 97
Crime, 111
Cross-caste and cross-class
    relationships (in U.S.), 57
Cuba, 68
Cultural styles, meaning of, 13.
    See also names of cultural
    styles
Cyprus, 119
Czechoslovakia, 67, 68

Daedalus, myth of, 71
Darwinian theory, 10
Defensive warfare, 141–42,
    143
"Depression-era children,"
    116–17
Depression of the 1930s, 136
Developmental change,
    commitment to (in U.S.),
    79
Diaspora, 16
Diathermal energy, 139
Dickens, Charles, 111
Dickson, Shannon, 74–75,
    107–8
Draft evaders, 105
Dreissig Jahre in der Südsee
    (Parkinson), 51
Drugs, 105

Dukhobors, 22–23
Dunkards, 22–23

Eastern religions, 130
Ecology, 153
Eisenhower, Dwight D., 140
Embryo's right to life
    movement, 112
Energy crisis, nuclear power
    and, 139–40
Environmental protection, need
    for, 144
Environmental Protection
    Agency, 107
Escherichia coli, 154
Eskimos, 98, 113, 154
    technology and
    ceremonialism, 54
Establishment, the, 65, 100,
    105, 112–13, 125, 130
Eta people, 16
Ethics, 85
Euthanasia, 126
Existentialism, 81

Foghat, 117
Food resources, development
    of, 69
Food stamps, 110
Fremont-Smith, Dr. Frank,
    140

Galileo, 27
Generation Gap, xvi–xx, 66, 67,
    76, 78, 95–119, 121,
    124–25, 137, 152
    domestication of, 95–108
    as a moment of opportunity,
    102
    nuclear debates and
    (1950s), 99–100
    slogan, 105
    unanticipated reverberations
    of, 109–19
    See also types of cultures

Geneva Summit Meeting
    (1955), 140
Genghis Khan, 65
Geographical migration, 62–63
Gorer, Geoffrey, 127
Gould, Richard, 24
Greece (ancient), 4, 123

Hair styles, 111
Hamlet of A. MacLeish, The,
    89
Hendrix, Jimi, 117
Hinduism, 21
Hiroshima, atomic bombing of,
    97–98
Hobbyhorse cult (in England),
    54
"Hot line" (between Moscow
    and Washington), 100
House of Lords (England), 82
Hutterites, 22–23
Huxley, Julian, 85
Hydrogen bomb, losing of (off
    Spanish coast, 1966), 100

Icarus, myth of, 71
Immigrant in time, concept of,
    70–71, 72
Incest, 24, 27
India, 16, 45, 126
Industrial revolution, 66, 69,
    104, 138, 139
Intergenerational relationships,
    postfigurative cultures,
    28–29
Ishi, 24
Islam, 21, 143
"Is Modern Man Obsolete?"
    (Cousins), 97
Israeli kibbutz, 40

Jackson State massacre, 97
Japan, 67, 68, 104
Jews, 16, 25, 29, 58, 61
Job scarcities (1970s), 106

Judeo-Christianity, 103, 123
Juggler of Notre Dame, The,
106

Kalihari Bushmen, 141
Kennedy, John F., 125
Kent State massacres, 97
Kibei Japanese (World War
II), 23
"Kidnapping" alienated
children, 128
Kinship systems, 4, 34
Kubrick, Stanley, 88

Language, 37, 40, 50, 77, 124
Law schools, admission
difficulties (1970s), 106
Led Zeppelin, 117
Lerner, Max, 65–66
Lidice massacre, 142
Life-support systems, turning
off (for hopelessly ill),
126
Linear purposes,
destructiveness of, 136
Lomax, Alan, 56
Long hair, 95, 106, 115–16
student expulsions, 116

McCarthy, Eugene, xvi, 113
MacLeish, Archibald, 89
Magic, 149–50
Manu people, xv, 50, 52–53, 89
Maoists, 88–89
Mao Tse-tung, 66
Marcuse, Herbert, 81
Maya Indians, 34
Mbaan (village elder), 51
Mead, Margaret, background
of, ix–x
Medical revolution, 69
Medical schools, admission
difficulties (1970s), 106
Melanesia, 20, 21. *See also*
names of people

Metraux, Rhoda, 6
Midwich Cuckoos
(Wyndham), 88
Military conquest, 40
Miller, Glenn, 117
Monastic orders, 132
Monocrops, 152–53
Mundugumor people, 26
Music, 105, 117–18
electronically amplified, 110
My Lai massacre, 142

Nader, Ralph, 107
Nagasaki, atomic bombing of,
143
Nanking massacre, 142
Napalm bombings, 112
National identity, sense of, 29
Nationalism, 67
Native Americans, 110
"Never trust anyone over
thirty" (slogan), 105
New Guinea, 3, 5–6, 18–20,
25, 26, 28, 30, 42, 50–53,
70, 71, 113, 121, 122
New Hampshire presidential
primary (1968), 113
Newton, Sir Isaac, 27
1960s perspective: 1970s
perspective. *See*
Perspective of 1960s;
Perspective of 1970s
Nixon, Richard M., 104–5
Northern Ireland, 68, 127
Nuclear-energy plants, 100
Nuclear family, 49, 53, 60–61

On the Beach (Shute), 100
"Open skies" speech of 1955
(Eisenhower), 140
Optimism, capacity for, 9–10
Orwell, George, 124
Overby, Pat, 118
Overpopulation, fear of, 140
Ozone layer, 144

Parkinson, Mrs., 51
Parkinson, Richard, 51
Peace Corps, 107
Perspective of 1960s, 3–91
  cofigurative cultures, 39–64
  postfigurative cultures,
    13–38
  prefigurative cultures, 65–91
  task of, 3–12
Perspective of 1970s, 93–157
  generation gap, 95–119
  new forms of commitment,
    121–32
  safeguarding diversity,
    147–57
  technology and, 133–45
Pidgin English, 50
Plutonium, 100, 127, 130,
  149
Poland, 55
Pollution, 137, 138
Population crisis, 126
Postfigurative cultures, 13–38,
  125
  absorption and identity,
    23–24
  children and, 25–27, 28, 29,
    32, 33
  conditions for change,
    15–16, 32–34
  conditions necessary for
    maintenance of, 35–36
  emigration and immigrants,
    31–33, 35
  gifted individuals, 27–28
  group membership, 16–17
  habitat, 16, 34
  idea of change, 85
  intergenerational
    relationships, 28–29, 34
  knowledge (among
    preliterate peoples), 29–31
  meaning of, 13–14
  need for older people, 15, 17

quality of timelessness, 22–23
sense of continuity, 14–15,
  17, 31
sense of national identity, 29
stability, 34–35
unanalyzed cultural behaviors
  and, 36–38
Prefigurative cultures, 65–91,
  148–49
communication with youth,
  77–78
development of, 83–91
dissidents (youth), 81–82,
  83
elders and, 75–78, 82
emergence of world
  community, 68–69
immigrant in time concept,
  70–71, 72
meaning of, 13, 83, 135
nature of change, 67–68
parents in, 79–82
rapid change and, 79–80
religion, 78, 79
right or wrong criteria, 78–79
sense of responsibility, 76
war weapons, 71–72
young generation and, 72–75,
  80–81

Rape, 111
Religion, 78, 142, 147, 150
Rhodesia, 68
Riesman, David, 66
Roman Catholic Church, 99
Rome (ancient), 4, 67, 123
Roosevelt, Franklin D., 131
Rothchild, John, 128
Runaways, 111

Saturday Review, The, 97
Science, 150
Science fiction, 71, 125
Scientific discovery, rate of, 78
Scientific revolution, 69

Sea explorations, interest in, 125
Seed banks, 153
Segregation, new kind of, 57
Self-consciousness, 68
Sex attitudes, 119
Sex lines, crossing of (in cofigurative cultures), 45–46
Shivistic rites, 21
Shute, Nevil, 100
Sikhs, 22–23
Sit-in demonstrations, 5
Slavery, 41
Solar energy, 139
Space explorations, interest in, 125
Sparks, Donald E., 115
Stein, Jim, 116–17
Street corner gangs, 126
Student activism, 110, 113
Student movements, decline of (1970s), 97
"Survival of the fittest," idea of, 10
Szilard, Leo, 8

Tambunam, village of, 5–6, 50–51
Technological change, 96
accommodation to, 66–67
Technology, 124, 147
based on cheap oil, 137–38
cost-benefit analyses, 138–39
diversity and, 153–56
hope within, 133–45
Television, 111, 112, 126
Television satellites, 69, 73

Teller, Dr. Edward, 65
Te Rangi Hiroa, 30
Tomi (political leader), 51–52
2001:A Space Odyssey (motion picture), 88

Undergraduate life, 107
University of California, 24
Urbanization, 152

Venezuela, 16
Vietnam War, 76, 105, 119, 142
end of, 106
use of defoliants, 72

Waddington, C. H., 78, 85
War weapons of extinction, 72
Windmill energy, 139
Wolf, Susan, 128
Woman's language (California Indians), 24
Woodstock (1970), 109
World community, emergence of, 68–69
World War I, 33, 97
World War II, 8–9, 22, 23, 36, 71–72, 143, 157
World-wide air travel, 69
Wyndham, John, 88

Yana Indians, 24
Yemenite Jews, 33
Youth or "teen-age" culture, 59

Zippers, 138
Zoos, 153
Zuñi Indians, 27